AN AFFAIR WITH A VILLAGE

Joy Hendry

Other Books by
Joy Hendry

Marriage in Changing Japan: Community and Society

Becoming Japanese: The World of the Pre-School Child

Understanding Japanese Society (5 editions)

Wrapping Culture: Politeness, Presentation and Power in Japan and Other Societies

Other People's Worlds: An Introduction to Social Anthropology (3 editions)

An Anthropologist in Japan

The Orient Strikes Back: A Global View of Cultural Display

Reclaiming Culture: Indigenous People and Self-Representation

A Beginner's Guide to Anthropology (with Simon Underdown)

Science and Sustainability: Learning from Indigenous Wisdom

AN AFFAIR WITH A VILLAGE

Joy Hendry

Map of Japan
and its major settlements

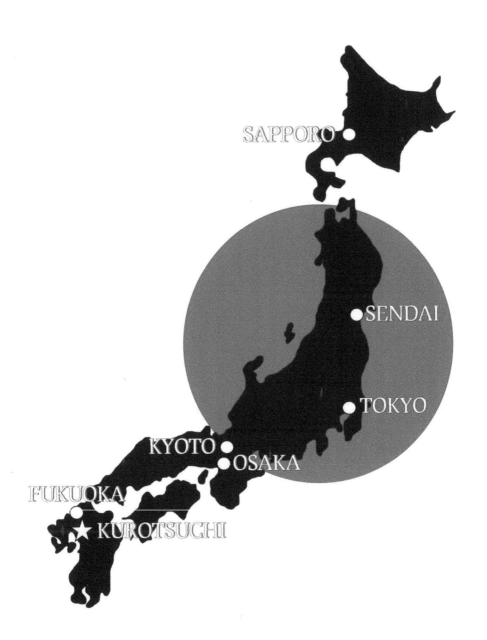

Contents

AN AFFAIR WITH A VILLAGE

Prologue

IN the autumn of 2019, I returned to the village in Kyushu, Japan, where I had worked over a period of nearly 45 years. I had spent one year, as an anthropologist, living close to the community, then returned for shorter visits, once with a BBC film crew, and twice with my children as they grew up. I had also returned several times to update a textbook I wrote about Japanese society, and the community I know so well in Kyushu has formed a basis for explaining albeit changing life in rural Japan. Altogether, this community has become so close to my heart that I feel almost as much at home there as I do in the countries – England and Scotland – where I was born and now reside for much of the time. On the other hand, I will always be an outsider, almost an intruder, because there is something slightly illicit about the work we anthropologists do.

Usually I stay with the family that had been my neighbours when I first lived in this rural community, and their home is very familiar. They treat me as one of their own, and two of their three now-grown children who live quite far away in Japan took the opportunity to visit during my recent stay. We have all visited each other over the years. One of the daughters became the first from the area to visit Oxford and Scotland, the parents came for a long trip, again to both places, once they had retired, and the son brought his new wife to my place in Scotland and they fell in love with both whisky and haggis! I have also visited their different homes in Japan, and every time we meet, wherever we are, we share a dish that my husband first famously tried out in Japan, namely roast beef and Yorkshire pudding! Chapter 3 includes the details of the reason it became famous.

However, the trip I have just made could be my last. In 1975-6, I made detailed family trees for each of the 54 houses and collected information about the origins and destinations of everybody who had moved in and out of the village. I had also made a large chart, showing how the houses in the village were, or were not, related to each other, despite predominantly sharing two surnames. This information has been used by me anonymously over the years in various publications, but after that it sat on a top shelf in my study in Oxford, and I decided it would be better off back in the village than gathering dust so far away, especially as I had agreed to change names when I referred to them in order to get access to some of the records, access agreed to by all the houses in the village at the time. Thanks to the Daiwa-Anglo-Japanese Foundation in London I was successful in a bid for a grant to travel back to the village to hand them over.

An added advantage was that my son, James, and his partner Nadine, were free to join me for this visit, and they filmed the whole process, smiling greetings at the surprised villagers as they came out to answer my calls at their doors. As I introduced them, the older inhabitants soon worked out that the man behind the camera had been one of the small boys that had accompanied my visits so many years ago, and whom few people in the village had seen since. My informal film crew recorded the handover of the documents, but we also talked to as many people as possible about their memories of my first and subsequent visits. The house I had lived in then has been flattened, but we walked around the space with the neighbours who had been children at the time, and verbally reconstructed some of the events that had taken place there.

It was a nostalgic occasion for us, quite emotional at times for my son, for I had lived there for some of the time with his father, whom we lost at much too young an age. However, I gained an enormous sense of satisfaction that I had managed to maintain a good relationship with a whole community over such a large part of my life. Things did not always run smoothly, and there has been heartbreak and frustration at times, but handing over these documents seemed to be a fitting way to complete an exercise that had formed an absolutely crucial part of my career working as an anthropologist in Japan.

While human beings usually find their most intense emotional experiences with other individuals of the same species, social anthropologists may encounter some of the same highs and lows with a wider section of humanity as they go about their chosen investigations. Thus, readers who have only the haziest idea of what social anthropologists get up to may well recognise aspects of the process, even down to the tinges of immorality and illegitimacy that occur and reoccur along the way. This book draws an analogy with such a personal engagement, as suggested by the title, from the experimental trysts of the first student forays into fieldwork, through a varied series of exciting but sometimes excruciatingly painful dalliances, to a long-term sense of moral obligation to the generations of villagers who have played the game so generously from their side.

The writing of this book was started after just one year working in the village and has been built upon more recently after nearly 45 years and eight further visits have passed. The style has softened a bit, but the early excitement has been retained, and the book now reflects some of the maturity of a long-term relationship between lovers, illicit or otherwise. The main purpose of the volume has now become less of an autobiographical confession than an attempt to explain a life choice about which the author remains passionate, and to inspire others who know nothing of the subject behind it to become curious and perhaps to absorb some of its value for themselves.

Chapter One

First Encounter

I DID not think Kurotsuchi very beautiful at first. Blue mountains rose softly against the sky beyond the neatly tiled rooves, but the village itself seemed untidy. A paved road ran straight through the middle, from east to west, and this appeared to form the chief residential section. The houses on the north side faced the road, and some were attractively built, but there was often an ugly vehicle parked in front, or a pile of old boxes. The south side was dull, and though there were sometimes doors to knock upon, the buildings were generally built to face away from this main thoroughfare. Later I would discover the quite complex reasons for this practice, and even later, my own prejudice in expecting the road to be a focus of interest. In fact, it petered out into a dirt track at each end, but the dirt track was regularly maintained, and led to the fields and the greenhouses which provided the workplaces of many of the inhabitants.

Then there was the usual approach from the main prefectural route that rumbled along a few hundred metres to the south. This was made along a third paved road, which passed a few unconnected houses, and then formed a T junction with the east-west one, but the first encounter with the village itself was to be found on the right-hand side, with a fishmonger's shop. This was a concrete construction, with large plain sliding glass doors, and usually fronted with a pile of packaging and other debris from the morning's delivery of fresh fish. The fishmonger was very friendly and always greeted me as I came

Entrance to the village, 1975

by. Next, an open gravel space, often occupied by a large lorry, and a couple of plain houses, before the tobacconist's shop, on the corner. This last was clearly embellished with signs and advertisements, and sported a row of gas cylinders, a main source of cooking power. It was also a main hub of activity, as people popped in and out throughout the day, and it turned out to be a good place to get my bearings and ask questions about general matters.

Across the street a tiny square opened into the village hall on the one side, and around the nearer corner, a public bath house. Two doors, set either side of the corner, flew to and fro from early evening as men and women separately made their daily ablutions. Inside, amidst the steam, they sometimes chatted over the wall, or passed soap between members of the same family, but inside the balmy chambers, there was a cosy intimacy. News spread like wildfire here, and secrets possibly meant for careful guarding slipped out as tired bare bodies relaxed in the scorching waters. In-laws, cousins, and long-standing friends of all ages scrubbed each other's backs, and rinsed away the grime of the day.

After supper, the village hall came alive, with meetings each night of the week, and strains of song, strings, or deep debate filtered through the doors into the pool of light outside. It was relatively easy to enter the bathhouse, to remove all my clothes and commune with a sea of strange bodies, but it took longer to feel comfortable entering a meeting, and even longer to understand everything that was going on. In any case, for many months, this evening village was alien territory for me. I lived over the main road in another community, and I had my husband at home, surely requiring attention after a busy day's work. I soon discovered that I could have a full bath at the end of the day, however, and make the 7-minute cycle ride home without losing the wonderful warmth of a soak in the shared hot water. Later I learned to time my bathing to coincide with the age groups – elderly women first, then the youngsters, and finally the middle-aged housewives whose work in the home kept them busy the longest.

At first, I simply wandered amongst the houses during the daytime, studying their external features while most of their occupants were working. I had plenty of time and space to draw a good map, and I systematically followed all the streams and footpaths as well as marking the arterial roads which lead on to further communities beyond. I was not without company, for the two shopkeepers were always willing to chat, and I even had to learn to divert the talkative wife in charge of the rice-hulling machine located to-

Mrs Komiya at the door of her rice polishing shop

wards the east end of the middle main road. She would pop out of her door as I tried to ride past on my bicycle, urging me to reveal where I was going, and offering all sorts of information. She was a good source of local knowledge, but I often didn't really know where I was going, and it took a while to realise that her question was simply a form of greeting.

I came across the ritual places in the village only gradually, despite my determined curiosity. The main Shinto shrine was easy. It occupies a

Tenmangu Shinto shrine at festival time

prominent place at the East end, its entrance clearly marked with a *torii* archway, and the whole compound raised above the surrounding paths. As well as the shrine buildings – a large one in the middle, and several smaller ones at the back – the villagers keep a row of swings in here for the children. After school this was another place to chat, then, and in the mornings, some of the younger infants would be brought in by elderly caretakers who could no longer contribute to the heavy work of the household. They could explain things to me though, and I discovered that the local protective deity was remembered at this place, that it was cleaned regularly by a rota of neighbours, and that an important festival was held here annually in the summer.

Another shrine, dedicated to the goddess Kannon according to its common appellation, was not only pretty well hidden from the main paths through the village but also much more puzzling to work out. Here a row of 13 Buddhist statues stand guard at the side of the path leading to the shrine building, but no one seemed able to tell my why they were there, or even very clearly to explain who they were. They were simply called the *Jûsanbutsu* (13 Buddhas), and it was said that pilgrims would come and pray to them on the spring and autumn equinoxes. This they did, and later I was able to learn a bit more about the statues, but for the time being it was never the site of any other activity.

More popular among the villagers, and probably more sacred too, is an empty piece of land behind the buildings towards the Western end of the village. I didn't find it for some time, for it is approached down a narrow path between two houses and it seemed intrusive just to wander along it, but this was a real hub of village life, even just to stop for a chat. Volleyball was one of the activities that took place there, and an intriguing croquet-like game known in Japanese as 'gateball', played in the summer at 5 a.m. by the elderly residents. These, I discovered much later when I also found that 5 a.m. was the most pleasant part of the hot summer's days, were practising to participate in tournaments with all the neighbouring communities.

There was a simple raised stage at one side of this space, and here concerts could be put on, I was told, but it was apparently only used seriously once a year for the festival of the *Shinboku*. This term literally means 'sacred tree', or 'god tree', and a twisted rope marked a particular tree as the one designated for this honour. It was not immediately clear why this tree was special, but I was told that there had been an

People chatting after work near the *Shinboku* sacred tree

● ● ●

4

enormous old tree on the same spot, one that required several people linking arms to reach all around its huge trunk. It had been felled by a single stroke of lightning during a terrible storm in the early part of the century, and the site was also often referred to in common parlance as *gorogoro-san*, an onomatopoeic local version of *kaminari-san*, or 'the god of lightening'. A small shrine to this god stands beside the tree and is tended regularly.

Shinboku sacred tree with shrine and bamboo

As I strayed out each exit from the houses of the village, I soon found more people to talk to, for the paths led into a mosaic of greenhouses, at this stage covered in polythene sheets which could be opened and closed according to the weather, and in which many of the villagers would be working. There they were cultivating chrysanthemums, first preparing the ground and planting, and then trimming each stem regularly so that it would yield only one huge flower. The 'houses' were lit during the night in the autumn so that the flowers would grow as they normally did in late summer and not

Chrysanthemum greenhouse with Tokiko and Tomoe holding her granddaughter at the back

Chrysanthemum greenhouse, lit up at night

Tea fields: picking the first tea of the season

reach their peak until the New Year period, when they were able to attract the best price.

There was also a hillside of tea fields, known as the *pairotto* or 'pilot', which had been carved some 15 years earlier out of ancient woodland that had supplied the villagers with wood and charcoal for fuel until they had transferred to the cleaner and more convenient bottles of gas that were delivered to their doors by the shopkeeper's son. A local politician – actually the one who introduced me to the village and who we will meet in the next chapter – had persuaded almost everyone to give up their share of this common land to tea fields, and they were now producing quite an abundant income for those who had invested in their own portions and the little windmills that kept away the winter frost.

An early attempt at participant observation had been here in these tea fields, where the first of the four annual crops, known as *shincha* or 'new tea', was in those early days picked by hand. I spent a spring morning working out in these fields and realised in just a few hours how hard life could be for my farming neighbours. The sun was already quite hot, and there was hardly any chat amongst them as we picked, so I decided it was not best use of my time, but we had a pleasant lunch together sitting under a temporary shady bower, and they sent me home with

Lunch with the tea-pickers after a morning's work

Transplanting rice by hand   Rice fields after transplanting

enough rice to last my husband and I a good month!

The third crop-growing process that could be observed was that very staple one of rice, and I was able to watch a few neighbours operating a basic machine together to plant the seeds in boxes, and then, when the seedlings had grown to a manageable size, taking them out to be spread into the carefully flooded rice paddies. My first trip coincided with the introduction of machines to transplant the seedlings in some cases, but I also caught on camera at least one field where the operation was still done cooperatively, by hand. The fields are also flooded in turn – another cooperative aspect of the work – and there was a festive air about this transplanting process (*taue*) which is recorded in local news and then national television throughout the country as each area put their staple crop into production according to the variable weather conditions, earlier in the south, and later in the north – and higher – regions.

There was also a local festival following the safe transplanting of the seedlings when neighbourhood groups gathered to fashion various objects out of last year's straw – an octopus, a set of *sake* cups, a bottle, and some other less obvious shapes – and these were hung up over the streams that supplied the flood

Kawamatsuri objects hanging over the stream

water that made the paddies effective. It was explained to me that the festival used to be to ensure that the water would keep coming but now they knew that their location pretty much guaranteed it, they would also pray for the safety of the children who might otherwise fall into the sometimes quite powerful torrents and be carried away. In fact, the only person who fell in during my stay was myself – but I will come to that story shortly. Meanwhile, the celebration ensured a day of rest and fun after the hard work of getting the rice seedlings into the fields, and the decorations hang above the streams for the rest of the year.

So here is the village that eventually I would fall in love with – nothing very spectacular at first – just a group of people going about their sometimes quite difficult lives, and I was the stranger who wandered in and began to observe them. They made me welcome, in fact they seemed quite to like my interference and curiosity; people in neighbouring communities would ask me why I had chosen that particular group, and sing the praises of their own villages, as if I could change my mind and move over to observe them. However, in those days an anthropologist usually stuck with one location and stayed there for a year or more – and after considering a few, I had made my choice. In fact, I would return again and again for a span of more than 40 years ... but let's not jump ahead.

Chapter Two

Introductions

MY arrival in the town of Yame in Japan's southernmost island of Kyushu was not made without introductions. Indeed, I had tentatively visited more picturesque villages in other parts of the country, but here I had been introduced by my supervisor in Tokyo to a Japanese anthropologist who had worked in a neighbouring community and he was willing to offer support. According to advice from my supervisor and anthropological colleagues back in the UK, I needed a place where I could get to know everyone well enough to learn to understand the way that their world worked, and as I had chosen marriage as a focus of interest, I needed people who were actually getting married in the area.

I had decided to go for a village as the relatively small and accessible unit, and in this period of quite strong urbanisation, I needed a place where young people were staying rather than taking off for cities as soon as they reached adulthood. The introduction of thriving cash crops such as chrysanthemums and tea had made this particular location quite appealing for its young people, and even many of those who went away to study or to seek adventure for a year or two seemed to find it more attractive than big cities, and would return when they were ready to settle down. Kurotsuchi had 54 houses and a population of 254 so it seemed a good size.

Matsunaga *sensei*, the anthropologist, took his introductory role very seriously, and he took me round to meet various local dignitaries before we even approached the village. One of these was the local member of the national parliament, a man named Toshiyuki Nishie, and it was in discussion with him that we actually chose the specific village. He had been the man behind the development of the tea fields mentioned in the last chapter, so he knew his constituents rather well. In turn they at-

Nishie san picking tea

tributed some of their recent affluence to him, so they were cooperative when he asked them to accept me as a visiting researcher.

Another very important character to whom we were introduced – and this after my husband had arrived, almost as if he validated my existence – was Mr. Sasabuchi, a big local businessman who owned a series of paper factories. He had somehow acquired a large empty house that had been abandoned by a wood merchant who left the area stealthily in the middle of the night (known in Japanese as a 'night flight' (midnight flit, or escape), and Sasabuchi was willing to let us use it. It was not a huge bargain, as we had to re-install services like water and electricity which had been cut off, but it made a beautiful home with some charming traditional features like painted sliding paper partitions between the main rooms and carved wooden divisions above them.

There was a proper Japanese front entrance, with a double set of sliding doors, and plenty of space for leaving one's shoes, an absolute necessity when entering Japanese living space (but look forward to a couple of fun stories about this area). The second set of doors led into an open area with *tatami* rush matting on the floor so that one could kneel and make formal greetings to visitors, and here I also kept the telephone, connected 'with wire' to others in the neighbourhood. The handsets called a number rather than ringing a bell so that they could be answered by

Our fieldwork house, with Dennis standing at the door

anyone in any of the houses on the system. There was a large kitchen for preparing meals and a well-timed visit to the spring sale at the famous Arita pottery market, not far away, as well as several loans from my good Tokyo friend Yasuro's mother in Saga, enabled us reasonably cheaply to equip ourselves with enough plates and bowls to serve ourselves and groups of visiting friends with quite handsome fare. We each had our own separate working area, there was a balcony for hanging out the washing, a pleasant garden with a pond sporting frogs, snakes and other smaller wildlife, and I even found myself with a personal dressing room (remember this, it also appears later in the story!).

Matsunaga *sensei* didn't know the people next door – our two houses were a little separate from others in the neighbourhood – but I went around quite soon after we moved in to ask about how to dispose of the rubbish we acquired. This was a good move, because Mr. Kumagai, who lived and worked next door, explained not only the waste disposal system, but also the Japanese custom of taking small gifts to one's new neighbours which ensured at least a tacit welcome from others around who might otherwise have wondered about the strange foreigners.

The Kumagais actually became the very good friends mentioned in the Prologue. They ran a paper-making business from a factory behind their house, with an office on the main road, so there was usually someone available if I needed advice of any sort. Dennis gave their school-aged daughters English lessons, and we received regular informal visits from their two-year old son, Atsushi. Even more importantly, Mr. Kumagai had grown up in the area and although our houses were only a few minutes' walk from the village I had chosen for my study, Mr. Kumagai knew all its residents very well.

This was because his father had been ostracised for a year by his own neighbourhood for bringing in machines to make paper in an area where it had traditionally been made by hand, and the children of his neighbours were instructed to mete out the same treatment to his 10 sons and daughters. The rules didn't spread over the village boundaries, however, so Kiroku (number 6 son and now my neighbour) actually knew his age-mates in my village as well as those in his own and experienced no pangs of village loyalty about spilling the beans when there were scandals to recount! In fact, there was later a fairly major scandal within his own family, and as I was party to it in a way, certainly aware of it, I learned first-hand about the strength of that local loyalty – but I jump ahead ... there were many more introductions to be made, and I include these initial details about my neighbour because they illustrate an interesting silver lining for my research in the clouds of his family's experience of disapproval during his childhood.

Matsunaga *sensei* was otherwise very thorough, despite his lapse about my immediate neighbour, and Dennis joked that he would soon be handing out our name cards to children and dogs he had included so many people in our round of introductions. An important person, again invaluable for the research, was the head of the chosen village, a position that is handed down through the established and respected elders of the community. The role of this person is to represent the village at a wider level, and he runs internal meetings and organises local tax-collection, as well as dealing with disputes.

To be introduced to him was essential, then, but an extra piece of serendipity occurred when he announced that his son, who had left to work in the city, was about to return to the community for his wedding. This was to be a big local event, and as soon as I explained my interest in marriage as a topic for research, he invited me to the festivities. This act of generosity on the part of the village head was to set a pattern for all future weddings because I was invited to every one, and treated just as the other guests, which gave me a most valuable insight into the way they worked.

His invitation also had another benefit, for although Dennis did not often accompany me on my research trips, he did agree to attend this first wedding and we were seated in an easily accessible location. This enabled all those present to approach us with one of the many circulating pots of Japanese rice wine and offer each of us what looked like the tiniest cup as a form of greeting. It was too early for us to have achieved any sense of how strong the *sake* was, or how to prevent too much being imbibed, and we got quite intoxicated. Indeed, it was after this occasion that I fell into one of those fast-flowing streams on the way home, luckily to be hauled out by my husband!

So why was this a benefit? Well, I felt a little embarrassed immediately afterwards, but having given this situation some thought, I think it was a very good opening event for us to attend. First, we were clearly displayed before all the important members of the community, we had been admitted to the fold by the man in charge, and we were quite obviously up for taking part in customary activities. Even more important, I now think, a wedding is an occasion for all kinds of banter not normally acceptable in everyday conversation, and we were subjected to quite personal questions about the most intimate parts of our lives.

At many Japanese weddings, at least in those days, the age-mates of the bride and groom would demonstrate in some quite graphic ways what is expected of them once they find themselves alone, so discussing fine detail of sexual encounters was quite appropriate. This is not usually something I – or indeed my husband – would discuss with anyone, let alone a room full of strangers, but a combination of excellent food, heavy doses of good strong *sake*, and a genuine desire to fit into the local community, meant that I probably revealed a lot more than I might otherwise have done. To be honest, I can't remember much of what I said, but no one ever refused to answer questions I put to them later, so perhaps we set another good precedent at that first wedding.

It was difficult at first to remember who everybody was, despite the 'manageable' size of the community, but another crucial introduction from Matsunaga *sensei* provided a wonderfully organised way to keep track of them all. Japanese towns and villages sport a comprehensive network of local police boxes, and in rural areas these constitute the homes in which individual policemen stay, so I was duly presented to the

The local policeman with his young son

equivalent of our local British bobby. He made a note of our details and inspected our credentials, but at the same time revealed that he had a comprehensive record, not only of the temporary foreigners, but of every single person who resided in the area.

In fact, this is common practice in Japan. Every house is registered with the police, and with the local government, but the local government is a bit more careful about revealing information – though, as I will describe later, we did eventually persuade them to show me their records too. Meanwhile, the policeman showed no such ethical restraint, and allowed me to sit in his parlour and copy into one of my notebooks details of every household in Kurotsuchi. This book has been with me ever since, and it is one of my most valuable possessions, for I use it every time I return to the village to remind myself of people's names, update details of births, marriages and deaths, and simply as an excuse to greet people at their doors and find out how they are.

To have this notebook also gave me an excellent reason to call on people right at the start of my project, for the police did not actually have totally accurate records, and my line of approach was to ask for an update that would reflect a current situation. I did need to meet everyone formally before I could proceed to 'study' a village, and this proved an effective way to do it. Most people were very happy to talk about their families, indeed one of the things I soon discovered was that the older families liked to introduce me to their ancestors as well as to the living members of their houses. Gradually I was able to build up a kind of village-wide family tree, where I could chart the links between families as well as the ancestral lines, and the elders particularly liked the idea that they would be remembered as they approached their own departure from the land of the living.

Most of the people in this community share only two surnames, and many of them could trace relationships between their houses, although the adoption of family names that in English we call surnames, is a relatively recent phenomenon among Japanese country folk. Thus all the Kawaguchi families are related only in that they share a connection with the land – and the name, 'mouth of the river' – suggests a choice reflecting that geographical phenomenon, though the situation was beyond living memory. The other local name – Shibata – was shared by people who could trace their common ancestry and they held an annual ritual to re-member their common forbears.

A few houses had other names, but not many, and they were still regarded as incomers though some had been there for a couple of genera-tions. The village where I stayed across the road had a more mixed popu-lation, but I never got to know the people there as well as I did the resi-dents of this chosen one. We did our main shopping over there and we got to know the shopkeepers, including one who 'rented' a black and white TV to us at no cost at all as 'everyone was now into colour TV'. We used the post-office regularly in those pre-internet days, and we took the train at the local station if we needed to travel further away. We also attended a big local festival, and my husband made a few friends on his side of the main road, including some who took us out on occasions, but my anthropological affair was with Kurotsuchi, and this is where I honed my curiosity and began to gather the materials I needed.

Chapter Three

Wooing

ANTHROPOLOGICAL investigation is quite different from those which have a series of questions ready once the people under study have been identified. The approach is much more subtle. Quite simply an anthropologist seeks to integrate into the lives of a group of people so that an understanding of their way of doing things can gradually emerge. Of course, one needs to explain in some way why such an approach should be necessary, and reference to language learning is one useful aspect of the endeavour, but my study was specifically to do with marriage and weddings, as everyone in the community now knew, so I needed to come up with some specific reasons for calling on people and getting involved in their lives. In some ways, this is a little bit devious because it is hard to know what to anticipate until one gains some initial information, so at first I felt as if I needed to woo people into accepting me. And like a wooing lover, I was easily encouraged by the slightest sign of friendship, but also vulnerable to even imagined rejection.

Fortunately, my initial plan to walk around with the policeman's list and visit every house in the village proved in almost every case to be a positive experience. In the Japanese fashion I had soon picked up, I would slide open an outside door and call out a greeting: *gomen kudasai* ('please to excuse me' is a rough translation). If there was no one in, there would be no reply, but otherwise a cheery face would usually appear at the door, and more often than not, I would be invited in. For people who carried out some of their work at home, I would simply be led into the working space, where no one seemed to mind a distraction; otherwise I was very often shown into the room set aside for receiving visitors, at least for my first visit; cushions would be lain out on the rush-matting floor, and a table set up where I could rest my notebook.

In this formal situation, the head of the house, usually a man, would come and sit beside me while one of the women would prepare some tea. There would be an exchange of greetings, I would outline my purpose for being in the community, answer questions about my own background, and open my notebook at the page I had prepared for this family. Men were often not as well informed as the women of the house, so they would call for help with my queries – names of relatives, birth-days, dates and details of weddings and funerals, locations of absent members of the family – and so forth. The occasion often drew in grand-parents and children as aspects they knew better were raised, and they were usually quite cheerful events, so it was rare that my next visit would not simply take place much more informally in a room where the family gathered anyway.

I tried not to outstay my welcome on any of these occasions, and I needed to get around the whole village, so it was not hard to find an ex-cuse to leave, and this first encounter with all the households of Kurot-suchi was actually quite reassuring. There was one family that was a lit-tle reticent about sharing information, notably about the location of one of their sons, and the policeman told me later that he had been impris-oned, so it was quite understandable that they did not want to say, and I did feel a little bad about having asked them at all. They had kept me on the doorstep, rather than inviting me in, and this did happen occasionally so I had just assumed the house was not in a state to receive visitors, or they were busy – I could easily imagine refusing entry to such a visitor myself – but I also needed to learn to be sensitive to non-verbal signals and respect privacy where people needed it.

During this early period, I made a detailed map of the village, gave all the houses numbers, and these were transferred into my notebook for cross-reference; it was useful to have several copies of these maps because the houses were grouped for various purposes: helping 'the three neigh-bours opposite and one on either side', as the Japanese saying goes; turn-ing out to sweep the streets and clean the streams; smartening up the shrines and hosting festivals; even tax-collecting was a village duty, and it was much easier to understand relations between houses once I had all these groups identified. Family relationships were also important, and these were a little harder to mark on the map, but I found a way to indi-cate where a younger son had within a generation moved out of the main home inherited by an elder brother and set up his own 'branch' house, and this was handy information when my focus moved more closely to understanding ritual occasions.

Another major task I decided to undertake was the drawing up of the massive family tree I mentioned, marking all the longer-term relationships between families in the village, and this seemed to delight especially some of the older members of the community. They were usually happy to talk of their own parents and grandparents, and they were very impressed when I could remember their names, some

The *butsudan* Buddhist altar

of which were quite long and splendid! Good for my pronunciation practice. The source of information further back than living memory was the Buddhist altar in the house, where ancestral tablets were stored, but the forbears were usually assigned a kind of collective ancestral category after 50 or 60 years, if the family remembered to make the transfer. Another complication was that people are given posthumous Buddhist names when they die, so it was a sort of cooperative venture within and amongst related families to get the anthropologist's household chart in order.

An interesting characteristic of family records sometimes emerged during these discussions, for there was an ideal way for a house to be passed down through the generations, and then there was what had happened in practice, which was not always the same thing. Most families owned land in the area which they farmed for rice, vegetables, or chrysanthemums, and it was necessary for a son who took the family name also to look after the fields. The land was scattered in different plots around the community, and a visit to the town hall had secured a detailed map of land of various types – rice fields were classified differently from land for flowers and vegetables, for example, and the emerging tea fields had taken over the category of common land that had in the past

The honey family

been used for collecting fuel. If the eldest son, or perhaps the husband of an eldest daughter, could not take care of all these lands, then another solution needed to be found.

One house in the village appeared to have no land at all; they made a living taking beehives out into woods which were still commonly shared, and then collecting and selling the honey that was produced by their bees. This family had a very interesting composition, as it turned out, and an interesting past as well. The oldest member of the family was apparently the granny, but she was not the mother of the head of the house, but the second wife of his father, whose first wife had run off and now lived in Hawaii. There had been no contact with the first wife since she left, and it seemed that it had been fine for the father to take another spouse to fill her place. There had even been another son, born to the now deceased father of the head and the woman who lived in the family home, but as he was the second son, he was not in line to inherit. Thus the family had split two mothers and their sons, but it followed a reasonably orthodox line of succession.

As for the reason that the family had no land, it seems that the grandfather of the present head had been an inveterate gambler, and he had lost all the family wealth playing a game known as *pachinko*. The house remained, and his son had taken it over and had the enterprising idea of the honey business, but there was a little house, hardly more than a hut, just outside the confines of the village where the old man had lived out his days with another son and a daughter who still lived there in some poverty. Actually this woman was often to be seen in the village stoking the fire for the village bath. This was a daily job officially transmitted by rota amongst the houses, but many preferred to pay this woman to do the job rather than to take time off from work which was probably bringing in more than they needed to settle her bills.

As I made my way around the community, people would frequently give me helpings of their crops: vegetables sometimes, fruit from their trees, and flowers as they came into bloom. The fishmonger at the entrance to the village would quite often send me home with fish, and I began to feel indebted. After all, I was the one taking up their time with my visits, yet my bicycle basket was rarely empty as I turned into our entrance, and Dennis and I were always well stocked with local produce. One day we decided to start inviting people around to share a meal, and as the fish had been the most substantial of our gifts we decided to ask the fishmonger. She had always been very friendly anyway, and she filled me in with all kinds of details about the other families in the community, so she came with her daughter.

The meal was a bit of a disaster because we had only Japanese plates, so we served soup and an assortment of Japanese-style dishes Dennis had put together, and then we brought out the rice. We didn't have a rice cooker, and I guess we had made it as Indian rice is usually served in the UK, a little *al dente*, which was definitely not the way it is cooked in Japan. Mrs. Nagashima – for yes, she came from one of the outside families, appropriately living on the periphery of the village – simply rose to her feet and took all our rice bowls back to the kitchen where she poured their contents back into the pan and began to boil up some more water to ensure that it would be properly cooked! It was deeply embarrassing, but it was something of an experiment, and we decided afterwards that dinner parties were perhaps not really the way to go!

There was one exception, when we decided to try and cook an English dish for our next door neighbours, the Kumagais, and this is really a story about the other community, but it is worth telling because it was something of a success, and it has now been handed down for years, as mentioned in the Prologue to this book. Japanese kitchens for the most part did not have ovens in those days, but the Kumagais had a sort of oven that sat on top of the gas ring that was standard issue, and we thought we might try and do a roast beef dinner. Dennis went out to do the shopping, and he started at the local butcher's where people usually bought thin slices of beef and other meats in small multiples of 100gms. He asked for 2 kilograms of beef. The butcher looked a little startled, but opened a cooler behind her and took out a side of beef which she held before her, asking him to say where he would like it to be cut. Dennis indicated a portion that he thought would be a good size (he was not one to stint on quantities where meat was concerned) and the butcher administered the chop. When she put the resulting piece of meat on the scales, it weighed exactly 2 kilograms!

I guess what followed could only happen in a small community, but before I ever made it back to the house, the word about Dennis's amazing ability to gauge the size of a piece of beef, as well as his insistence on buying such a large portion, had spread abroad. I first heard the story as I popped into the local convenience store to pick something up at lunchtime, but queries about the supper that was in store continued for the rest of the day, and the Kumagais themselves never forgot. To this day, some forty-odd years later, and thankfully now with the assistance of good electric ovens, we celebrate our reunions not only in their main house, but in those of their married children, and in mine in the UK, with a roast beef dinner, though in Japan I still sometimes have to improvise a bit about containers to cook the Yorkshire puddings.

My attempts to woo the people over in the community of my research were not all good, and another mistake I made was when I went around our garden and picked large quantities of a plant known as Japanese rhubarb. I had been told that it was edible, and we had tried it out, with sugar, just as one cooked rhubarb at home. I made bundles of the plant, and carried copious quantities in my bicycle basket, delivering it, just as I had received vegetables, fruit and so forth, to the people to whom I felt most indebted. Some were polite for a while, they always seemed pleased that I had gone to the trouble of bringing them a gift, but eventually someone took me aside and explained that this plant was really a weed. Yes, it was edible, but it wasn't very nutritious, and it didn't make a good present!

I guess it was actually a good sign that my new friends understood my research well enough to know that I would want to have such a thing explained to me, and also that they felt close enough to tell me to my face about my mistake. Eventually I found another way to thank people for their time and their kindness because in those days, photographs were not as readily available as they are now; film needed to be developed and printed, and prints were a little expensive. So I would distribute photographs I had taken of people at the various village events I attended and these seemed to go down well. It also gave me an opportunity to call on people to deliver them, and this was an excellent way to keep in touch. Much later, I discovered that people were actually happier that I became indebted to them than they to me, but I am jumping ahead again – the force of this discovery took a lot longer than what I have described as the wooing process, and it will be revealed in due course.

Chapter Four

Building Relationships

A S time went by, I began to build up closer relationships with members of the community, gradually in many cases, but mostly quite encouragingly. Some people were more friendly and open to explaining what they were doing as they went about their lives than others. The shop-keepers were simply around more, as was the woman who ran the rice-hulling machine – she was so much in evidence that I nicknamed her Mrs. Ubiquitous, and she can be found in my notes and diaries under that name! A third opportunity for getting to know people better was if they were involved in a special occasion of some sort. Weddings were of course prime in this regard, and I was invited to other celebrations, such as the taking of a baby to be introduced to the village guardian deity at the main shrine, and a particularly helpful example was when a house was being rebuilt, for in those days all the neighbours turned out to help, and there was much celebration.

It was also really encouraging for me when I was asked along to meetings of the groups that the villagers were divided into, some for keeping the place in order, or ensuring its safety, others largely for social reasons. When I was allowed to sit in a room of people going about their affairs, I could observe and listen without feeling obliged to ask questions, and this is actually one of the best ways of learning for an anthropologist, for we don't know what we don't know when we start our studies, and things emerge under these conditions which we might never have thought to ask about. As time went by, I would actually feel quite upset if I learned of meetings like this to which I had not been invited, though of course there was no intrinsic reason why people should feel obliged to ask me.

A couple of early really helpful events were brought to my attention by Mrs. Ubiquitous, so I should not be critical of her ubiquity. The first was a gathering of neighbours to sow the rice seeds in trays, these to

Sowing the rice seeds in trays with Mrs Ubiquitous

be laid out to germinate before the seedlings are planted in the fields. It was a jolly occasion, and informal chat accompanied the supervision of a fairly basic machine that distributed the seed evenly as the trays passed through. Planting out was done in rotation to share the water evenly between the fields, but the same group of neighbours gathered at the end to make the straw objects to be hung about the streams,[1] and this was again an occasion of much cheerful chat-ter, especially when the octopus was achieved with eight people plaiting the straw in unison to create the legs! The photograph I took once the job was complete is iconic in a way, but some people look as if they still found my presence a little odd!

One member of that neighbourhood invited me into her home on more than one occasion, because she worked there, and she liked to have company. Satsuki's husband was the local carpenter, and he was training a couple of apprentices, so she took care of this extended family during the day and had three children who returned home after school. She was a wonderful help in answering questions I might have about details of betrothal and marriage arrangements, and on the page opposite her fami-

Weaving the octopus for *kawamatsuri*

Neighbourhood photograph at *kawamatsuri*

[1] See illustration on page 7.

ly information, I have a list of the costs of all the elements of a wedding – the 'nail tea' that seals a proposal, the engagement ring and the wedding ring (both introduced relatively recently from the West), the substantial selection of betrothal gifts, the receptions, the garments to be purchased, the honeymoon, and the thank-

Hideshi Shibata's betrothal tea

you present for the go-between. Details of how these costs are shared between the families are also included, as is the relationship of the total to the annual earnings of the families involved – pretty much the same as it turns out, although annual earnings vary for the self-employed which many of the villagers are. This was the kind of crucial information that was really helpful to my research, but which few would have the time or inclination to share with me.

One of the weddings that took place while I was there was of the son of a family that lived on the other side of the main road, and for this too, I collected a huge amount of detail, as well as making very good friends with the young man in question. Hideshi and his family were again open to all my inquiries, and they invited me to the preparatory parties as well as to the wedding. He also laid out the betrothal gifts he was preparing to deliver to his bride to be and explained the symbolism

Hideshi's other betrothal gifts, including bream and kelp

of the various components – packets of 'poor tea' because it can only be served once, and a bride should only leave home once (the same word is used in each case), a huge sea bream because the Japanese word for bream (*tai*) is part of the word for congratulations (*omedetai*), and a kind of edible kelp, because its name (*konbu*) can also be written as 'child-bearing woman'. Other items express a wish for health, wealth and long life for the couple.

The honey family also lived in that neighbourhood, and they invited me up to the place in the hills where the hives were being kept at the time. We left before dawn, and it was an eerie sensation being in the woods when they lit small fires to smoke out the bees, just as the sun was breaking through the surrounding bamboo groves. Back in their home, the granny demonstrated the extraction of royal jelly from the honey that is collected, and I was able to watch the rest of the process as they prepared the honey for sale. The family had only one son, and he was a student at Fukuoka University during the time I was there, so he gave me a lift one day to visit my anthropology mentor Matsunaga *sensei*. On the journey we had quite a chat about this young man's aspirations for the future. He would be in line to inherit the business, but at that time neither he nor his parents knew what he would do once he graduated, and when I left, it was still uncertain. In the long run, this family proved to be one of the most successful in the village, as we shall see in due course!

Neighbourhoods were only one form of grouping within the village, others were based on age and occupation, and some had more specific roles as well. One of the most important of these was the care of the village fire engine, its maintenance and regular testing, and members of this group also needed to be ready to run out from whatever they were doing in case of fire – or other emergency. The group was a sort of age grade too, as it consisted of young men, most of them recently married, a step which demonstrated a commitment to stay in the community, and they also needed to be working in the vicinity. This group met once a month to check on the machine and carry out their duties, but they would then stop for a drink and a chat together, and they didn't mind the anthropologist sitting in the corner, so I got to spend a regular spell of time with them.

The Youth Group was also quite active, this time boys and girls who had graduated from school, but lived and worked in the village, and one of their roles was to make preparations for the festivals. They plaited quantities of straw to make the big *shimenawa* that marks the entrance to the shrine, for example, and they also created decorated staffs to be offered to the deity and then carried from house to house to share out the blessings. They brought one to my house too, despite being over the border in another shrine district, and they refused the 300 yen everyone else was paying, so I felt like an honorary member of the Kurotsuchi god's domain. Again, their meetings were

Youth group plaiting the *shimenawa* for summer festival

cheerful and fun; in some parts of Japan they would apparently provide an opportunity for young people to meet each other and to choose partners to marry, but the custom here was to marry out of the village, so they were more like an extended kin group.

There was a children's group too, and Satsuki's friendly daughter, Chika, who was one of the seniors at the time, would make sure I knew about their activities. They were the primary school children who met every morning to walk to school together, so they were well known to each other, and before the school holidays they met to discuss how they would pass the time. This was an interesting occasion because the children themselves suggested behaviour that was thought to be dangerous or annoying, and a list of such activities was printed and distributed, as a kind of group commitment to behave well when there was no school. There was an outing, which was a lot of fun, and the school sports day was a particularly good occasion to support the village and chat to the parents, who took time off for it. Dennis came along to that one and did a great demonstration of controlling a football as he dribbled it all around the ring. I always found the children wonderfully cooperative and interesting to talk to – they had few reservations about sharing what they knew about village life, and of course, they knew a lot.

I discovered age to be an important factor in the lives of Japanese people in general, and especially in the case of children coming through school, who learned to respect their seniors and take care of their juniors. The Japanese word for 'friend' is *tomodachi* but it has further implications in Japan where it is only used to apply to people of approximately the same age. In this part of Japan, there was a further reminder of this principle, for there were also groups, known as *tomodachi-ko*, which comprise people of a similar age who save money at regular meetings to go on outings together. I was invited to one which comprised five farming women who each host a dinner once a year, save a sum they bank, and then together visit a hot spring during a slack period in the agricultural cycle. Most of the groups are gender specific, those of the girls named after a rite associated with sewing, while the boys save and plan for a period away climbing a nearby mountain peak together. The boys' groups continue if they stay in the village, whereas young wives need to form new ones when they marry.

Mrs. Ubiquitous called me along to an event which raised the subject of age-mates quite naturally, and this was the presentation of a new baby to the local guardian deity. The custom is found throughout Japan, and very often one set of grandparents will send a beautiful kimono to be

worn when the child attends a festival at a slightly later age, but in time for the baby to be wrapped in it to be taken to the shrine at around 30 days. The occasions I witnessed actually involved both sets of grandmothers, along with the mother, who set the baby down before the altar, and if it is too quiet, they pinch it to make it cry so that the deity would notice its new charge! Other small children would be brought to the shrine – by their grandmothers very often – as this was, Mrs. Ubiquitous explained, an opportunity for them to meet their new

Grannies arriving at the shrine with a new baby boy

ages mates. The baby would be unwrapped and shown off, and

some rice with azuki beans to mark the celebration would be shared.

It was also Mrs. Ubiquitous whose family decided to rebuild their house while I was working in the village, and this decision enabled me to attend several very interesting events, and to spend time with villagers as they worked and cele-

Children waiting at the shrine to see the new baby

brated the procedure as it evolved. In those days, it was usual for neighbours to take time off from their usual work to help each other rebuild their houses, and as the houses are mostly built of wood, I was told that it was common to rebuild, or at least refurbish them substantially, approximately every 60 years. Thus, in a continuing family, passing the property on along with the family business, this rebuilding would happen once in a generation, and each family in the neighbourhood could call on the others to help in some kind of rotation without incurring a huge cost.

Professionals were required to prepare the materials, of course, and the most important of these was the carpenter, whose role in Japanese translates literally as 'great craftsman' (*daiku*). Together with the family involved, he makes a plan for the new house, taking into account various rules of geomancy, and then he cuts the wood for the framework into the

Housebuilding with neighbours taking part

required lengths, and times his delivery to coincide with an auspicious day when the neighbours can be there to put them together. In fact, two separate days are needed from the neighbours, for they came first to dismantle the old house and then later, when the space is cleared, to construct the new one. It was a most impressive sight to see the men climbing and cooperating to carry out these tasks, and the women gathered at a long makeshift table at the side to prepare food for them all. The walls were afterwards made by professionals, and the tiled roof again required specialist work. I was a generation too late to see the thatching that had preceded this type of roofing.

There was considerable ritual to be observed during this whole process, and each stage offered chances to be present, to observe, and to learn. Once the ground was cleared and prepared, a Shinto priest is called, and a temporary shrine set up in the space. Offerings are made to the deities affected, and the priest blesses the land, the family and the carpenters. Part of the procedure involves the shaking of a staff decorated with paper strips over the participants, and the priest insisted that I be included. I feel sure he shook his staff more fiercely over the unknown foreigner than anyone else! The most auspicious day for this house was not a convenient one for the neighbours, so one post was erected on that day in the northeast corner, otherwise known as the 'demon's gate corner' (*kimonzumi*), the explanation revealing all sorts of fascinating information about customs related to the geomancy of laying out a house, and the use of space.

On the day of the actual construction, all the participants were given towels known as *hachimaki*, died red at one end, to wrap around their heads – a symbol of work with ritual significance – and they were

Shinto priest performing the rite before a new house is built

also given a taste of the rice, salt, fish and *sake* that had been offered to the deities as a rite of protection against the dangers of this work. It was extraordinary to me to see the whole house take shape in one day, but it did, and once the roof had been put in place the following day, there was a further ceremony that brought out the whole village to celebrate. This involved the house head and the chief carpenter carrying out another rite at the pinnacle, with the same elements of rice, salt, fish and *sake*, and then hurling down large quantities of rice cakes, some of them prepared with small coins in them. Everyone scrambled for the cakes, so it was a very jolly occasion, described variously as protecting the family from misfortune, giving the new house a birthday, and enabling all the neighbours to join in. Everyone in the village sent gifts to the family, along with their aid, so it was truly a community occasion. It was also a wonderful learning experience for the anthropologist!

Chapter Five

The Family Register – and Greetings

NOT all the events in the village were celebrations, of course. One day, I noticed that one of the houses was displaying large colourful wreaths, mounted on stands, in full view of passers-by. The flowers in the wreaths were shades of blue and green, unlike similar red and orange ones I had seen in the town, announcing a new business. It was soon explained to me that this was an indication that someone in the family had died, raising the important and sometimes quite subtle division between markers of events to be celebrated and those to be mourned. I realised that I needed to learn the system (including colours) underlying the expression of these differences, and even more importantly, appropriate ways of behaving under these opposing circumstances. The person who had died was a son who had left the house, so I didn't know him, but it was a tragic situation for the family as he had been killed in an accident, and I had no idea how to react should I meet them. As it turned out, much of the appropriate reaction is quite clearly decided, and people were willing to explain the customary practice to me, so wakes, funerals, and the memorials that follow, did now offer another set of ritual events to share and to observe, although I felt even more of an intruder when those involved were suffering such a personal loss.

House with wreaths to announce a death

**Lanterns for a funeral at the household
Buddhist altar**

Close neighbours generally come out to help with the practical details associated with marking a death, it was explained, such as erecting the wreaths, which were sent by the company the young man worked for, and making preparations for the funeral. This leaves the relatives free to engage in the other numerous aspects of ritual to be observed. Word is put out throughout the village, and representatives of most houses drop by on the evening of a death to express their sympathy. Rituals of mourning are usually carried out in front of the Buddhist altar[2] in the house – the *butsudan* – which is where the ancestors are remembered. Beautiful lanterns are set up in front of the altar when someone has recently died, but the first of the day's rice is presented for years afterwards, as are other offerings such as fruit, bottles of *sake* and other things that the deceased person liked. The Buddhist altar is the place for communicating with ancestral members of the family, and sometimes visiting relatives will arrive and pay their respects to their forebears before greeting the living members of the household. Another interesting custom is to open the Buddhist altar when discussing matters relating to the house, so that the ancestors can be present.

Soon I realised that understanding rituals associated with death and the memorials which take place at intervals after a person has died, and indeed, the attendance at weddings and other family celebrations, all require a good understanding of family relationships as well as those between neighbours and age-mates within the village. Although young people tend not to marry members of the same community, a few have done. Also, as the custom is for only one son to inherit the family line, several of the houses are related through having formed branches of a

---

[2] See illustration on page 19.

larger house in the past, when the land may be divided. A daughter may even stay in the house and the family adopts a husband for her if there is no male heir. As explained earlier, all the families with one of the main surnames in the village are not only related, but celebrate their common ancestral heritage once a year, and several of those with the most common surname are related too. It was helpful then that I had decided to set about making family trees for each of the houses as well as the larger chart I had already initiated showing which were related to each other, and through what kind of connections.

As I mentioned, the older members of some households were not only willing but delighted to help me with this; they liked to talk about their parents and grandparents, long gone but still in their memories, and indeed, often in photographs above, and almost always named on tablets known as *ihai* inside the *butsudan* altars. If they weren't in their own Buddhist altar, it was because their house had branched off from another, and they would be in the main house, so that link would be made clear. However, this method was only partially successful. Most of the older women, now sometimes widows, had married into the house where they lived, and although they could recite the names of ancestors they had cared for through life and death, they would claim little knowledge about those who preceded them. In other houses, people neither had the time nor the inclination to engage in this task. When someone dies, memorials are held at certain fixed intervals for up to 50 years, after which a celebration is announced and the deceased person moves to a general rather than a specific category of ancestor, but some families fail to complete the full cycle if they don't really remember an individual who died, and so that one would join the general category earlier.

I discussed this problem with Professor Matsunaga, who advised me to go to the City Hall where family records have been kept since the end of the 19th century, a time span that we thought would help me to complete the task I had set myself. This advice proved interesting in various ways. I had already made contact with some of the civil servants in Yame City Hall, and they had supplied me with maps and information about land types and ownership. They had been extremely helpful, and interested in my work, and in theory at least were willing to help me access these records as well. However, family records are notoriously private in Japan because they used to indicate membership of particular social classes, and discrimination on the basis of social class had now been outlawed. Many of the records have been amended, but when I did eventually get to see them, the administrator in charge laughingly showed me that it was still possible to see that crucial part of the entry even though it had been erased in two different ways! Actually, this issue was of interest to me anyway, because people like to find out about the social origins of families into which they are thinking of marrying, especially if they are from a formerly outcaste class, but for the present purpose of establishing relationships this wasn't really relevant.

After some consideration, and consultation up and down the hierarchy of the City Hall, it was decided that I could study the records in the interest of my research, if three conditions were met. The first was to gain the signature of my supervisor, since I was only a student, and they agreed that this could be Professor Matsunaga, who had actually accompanied me when I first inquired about the possibility. He needed to have the letter he signed stamped by his university, but thankfully I didn't need to write to Oxford as well, as this could have taken a very long time in those pre-fax and internet days. The second sounded onerous and somewhat nerve-wracking, as it required me to gain agreement from each of the houses involved. However, making the list and going after signatures turned out to be a blessing in disguise, as I shall shortly recount. The third was that I was to change the names of people if I used their records in my publications, and this I assured them was not a problem as I had planned to give members of the village anonymity anyway, when I heard that another village in Kyushu studied by an anthropologist had been inundated with unwelcome visitors. Mr. Fujita in the Town Hall should not remain anonymous, however, as he was incredibly helpful in this and all other matters and will reappear in a later chapter (read on, dear reader!).

What then was the silver lining to the cloud of needing to consult all the houses in the village? It did become a cloud for me for a while, because I wondered whether anyone would be upset at the idea of my reading their family records, which seemed to be such private things, and if only one house disagreed, I would not be able to proceed. One evening after I had mentioned it to a few people, I was watering the tiny garden we had at the front of our house, and the husband of the shopkeeper stopped as he was driving by. He had probably only planned to greet me, as it turned out, and I may have used the expression Mrs. Komiya used so often and asked him where he was going, but he put the wind up me at the time because he replied that he was off to see Mr. Nishie, the councillor who introduced me to the village. The local member of the na-tional parliament, a former landowner, basically a man of power in the area (as the Japanese describes such people), the shopkeeper's husband could have had all kinds of business with him, but I spent a night worry-ing! The shopkeeper's wife came, I knew, from a family that was sent to Manchuria during the Japanese occupation there. Could that be a prob-lem? Could my interest in family history ruin the good relationship I had hoped I was building up with the village focus of my research?

Not at all, as it turned out, for having a legitimate excuse to visit all the houses again coincided with the big summer festival of *Obon*, when members of country homes who have moved away return to greet their ancestors, and everyone takes a break from work. This is a mid-year gathering when people all over Japan visit their family graves, and bands gather to play in town and city squares cleared so that people can dress in cool summer kimono known as *yukata* and dance together on a summer evening. I had experienced this with my friends in Tokyo, but I didn't know how it would be celebrated in the countryside, so it turned out to be a great time to call on people and see what they were up to with their usually distant relatives. As it happened, many were at home, and some-one from every house signed my list, and often enough invited me in to share their activities as well.

It was not always a happy occasion, for in some houses, one of the people they were remembering had died only recently, and this was known as *hatsubon*, the 'first bon' after a death. In this village the beauti-ful lanterns were set up again in front of the Buddhist altar, and when I called on the family that had lost their son not long before, I naively commented on their beauty. The elder brother shook his head sadly and said that this was not the kind of beauty people really wanted in their homes. Nevertheless, they invited me in, and I was shown how to kneel before the altar and say a prayer for the soul of the person who had died. We spent some time talking about the young man they had lost, what he had liked and how he had lived and played as a child, so it was a good opportunity to express my sympathy in a way I had not known how to do when I first heard of the tragedy.

This was a good lesson because I now knew how to behave when someone dies in a house, and the *Bon* period offered the opportunity to put this learning into practice. Three houses had lost a member that year, and I soon discovered another custom, which is that every house in the village calls round at this particular time with a gift of a few hundred yen wrapped in an envelope displaying the same colours of mourning that had been displayed on the wreaths that announced the death. Close relatives give more, and some offer noodles called *somen* that are eaten cold in the hot summer weather. All approach the *butsudan*, light a stick of incense, and ring the little bell there in order to say goodbye to their former neighbour. It seemed at first a little morbid to visit houses in order to pay respects to their dead, but it was a practice I started at this time, which was quite clearly appreciated by the families concerned, and possibly also brought them a little comfort. Over the ensuing years of visits, I made a point of calling at the houses where someone had died, and of course, this was particularly appropriate where I had known and worked with the deceased person when they were alive.

Nōkotsudo building, where ashes of the ancestors are stored

Where no one had recently died, there was more of a festive atmosphere at *Obon* because families were being reunited with the offspring who had left to make lives elsewhere, and several invited me in as I called for their agreement to let me study the family records. I demurred a couple of times, but as that seemed disappointing to people who perhaps wanted to show off their resident foreigner, I began to accept and spend time around their tables, sharing tea and fruit and all manner of useful information which emerged during the conversation. In fact, our house was

Lanterns mark the site of an old castle for dancing at *Bon*

very close to a building where ashes are stored, so I could also observe people making visits there, and later dancing as they had done in Tokyo.

One final interesting aspect of the exercise, apart from the eventual work I sat down to do in the Town Hall, was the way in which people approached the signing of the agreement form. Actually, signing was a relatively new form of agreement in Japan, where names are written in the Chinese characters chosen for them at birth, and the stamping with a registered seal was required to complete the job. In all houses, only one person was needed to accomplish this task, for it was a family register in which the generations are listed together. I had wondered whether both the head and his successor would be needed, in most cases men, but in practice a woman of the house could do this, and in one case a youngster took on the job. The seal was a household object, representing the whole house, and as long as the person stamping could write the name of the head, it seemed to be enough. Interestingly too, some people needed to practice the writing of the characters before they would commit them to my form, and one or two even asked me for confirmation that they had used the right number of strokes!

All in all, this exercise in coming to meet and greet the distant, the deceased, and even the ancestral members of the village families at this special midsummer festival when they all come together, seemed to bring me closer to them as well, and I began to feel reassured that my presence was not as unwelcome as I had sometimes worried it might be.

Chapter Six

A Sudden Shock

O F course, coming close to people does in the long run bring pain as well as pleasure, as my story will eventually reveal, but I was totally unprepared for the first example of the negative side of this experience. Even in the period leading up to *Bon*, I had got to know some families better than others, and there were a few individuals who I began to think of as friends. My own age-mates stood out in this respect of course, especially the girls, but some of the younger boys had called round on us as well. Dennis was always polite at least, sometimes quite charming, but he didn't really enjoy sharing me with a whole village, so I didn't encourage such visits. He had a circle of friends – mostly students of English – in the community where we stayed, and I think they were enough, as he did also have his own academic work to do.

This was also one of the reasons why I chose the title of this book as 'an affair' with a village as I did sometimes feel torn about my conflict-ing loyalties, and although Dennis knew perfectly well what I was doing, he did sometimes express a bit of jealousy about the time my work there took up. Some of the people who came round were also unconvinced that it was I, a woman, doing the research, rather than simply collecting mate-rial for my male partner/co-researcher, who must be the real scholar, so I think they came to check him out, which made matters even more un-comfortable for him. He did acquire enough Japanese language to do the shopping and enjoyed *sumo* wrestling so much that he picked up enough to understand and mimic the often very curt responses of the wrestlers when they were interviewed, which sounded so impressive that local people thought he knew more than he did. However, it was not his *forte* and we both got tired of the need to translate and explain everything be-ing discussed.

One of the families I got to know well gave us no such hassle. The grandfather remained curious about how a woman could be working for

Baba granddad at his tomato greenhouse

a doctorate, but he always stopped to chat anyway, and I was often invited round to their house. The family consisted of a set of grandparents, still active with the farm and domestic work, the eldest son Sadami, his wife Kiyoka, and three daughters, Sumiko, Atsuko and Aiko, all of school age. They were very good at answering questions that had occurred to me elsewhere, but they were also all simply friendly and fun. Around the time of *Obon* (the date of which varies slightly in different parts of the country to avoid total gridlock on the roads and railways) there is another event called *Tanabata* held annually on the seventh day of the seventh month (July 7th), but again adjusted according to farm work, and they invited me to come and see what they were doing.

Tanabata is also known as the star festival because it is based on a Chinese story about two stars, Vega and Altair, that represent a cowherd and the Princess Orihime, a weaver. They fell in love so deeply that they abandoned their work to be together. The father of the princess separated them, but because his daughter was so upset, he allows them to meet once a year on that day. The story recounts that they are separated by the Milky Way, which is difficult for them to cross, so a flock of magpies comes and builds a bridge, but only if the sky is clear, so it is said that everyone in Japan hopes for good weather that day. Children are also encouraged to write wishes on colourful slips of paper and hang them on bamboo branches.

Sumiko, Atsuko and Aiko invited me round to join them as they wrote their wishes, and as one of their father's brothers was visiting with his family, they had a cousin with them too. We had a lot of fun thinking of things we would like to wish for, and they carefully wrote them out, and hung them on the bamboo branches that had been prepared. They had each also prepared long streamers to celebrate Tanabata, using their

• • •

best calligraphic skills to write the characters for *Ama no Gawa*, the Milky Way, and signing them with their names and school class. As was customary, we ate large slices of watermelon, and this fruit is so associated with Tanabata, that they had also drawn coloured

Baba daughters with the tanabata pendants

pictures of watermelon to hang alongside their wishes. It was a lovely afternoon and the last time I saw these girls truly happy.

A few days later, I went off to visit an old friend in another part of Japan. I had also invited a couple of friends from Tokyo to come and stay with us, so I was temporarily distracted from thinking about the village as I made the house ready for visitors, and caught up with people from an earlier Japanese stay. We needed to clear space, organise and air the futons they would use for sleeping, and give our bathroom a good clean. It was summer and pretty hot, so not much bedding was needed, but the bath certainly needed to be in good working order.

The day I got back from being away, I almost didn't go over to the village, but I thought I would just show my face in case anything was being organised that I hadn't heard about, and I set off around mid-afternoon. I was cycling alongside a rice field, a short-cut I often used, when one of the men I knew quite well came running out of his greenhouse, waving frantically. He looked very serious, and his news was a bit difficult to understand, so I had to ask him to explain one or two of the words he had used. What he was telling me was also such a shock that I wanted to make absolutely sure I hadn't got it wrong, but basically, it was straightforward. Sadami, who was 37 years old at the time, had set off early for work a couple of mornings before, and had simply dropped dead by his greenhouse.

I was stunned by the terrible news, and asked for further details, but none seemed to be well known. There was speculation about whether it was a heart attack or some kind of aneurism, but the small group of people who had soon gathered to tell me, were sure that he must have been working too hard – a phenomenon quite often reported in Japan, and this village was renowned for its hard-working occupants. But Sadami had been 37, I argued, and his father and mother also worked hard; how come he had been the one to die? I had watched him climbing nimbly to help his neighbours build their new house only a few weeks before.

Someone dying at 37 is of course shocking, but I had got to know this man and his family rather better than many others, and I found the news really difficult to assimilate. The way the consequences were being recounted was also quite shocking to me, although it did teach me a huge amount in a short space of time about how the family is conceived in this rural part of Japan. No one said, 'poor Kiyoka losing her husband', 'poor children losing their father', or even 'poor mother and father, losing their son'. The immediate reaction was concerned with the 'house', the *ie* as it is called in Japanese, meaning the people who comprise it as well as any building they might share. 'Who will take over the house now', they asked, 'how will the family carry on?' Sadami had two brothers but they were doing well in jobs in the city, and they were not qualified to come back and work on the farm.

In the short term, Sadami's age-mates organised the harvest, and they and the immediate neighbours helped the family cope with all the things that they could not do alone. Kiyoka herself was later to be seen driving a tractor. But the death was a disaster for the household, and no one quite knew what would happen. My own reaction was to want to go and hug those lovely children, and sit down and cry with Kiyoka, but this was Japan, and to be honest, despite learning some ways of dealing with death only a few weeks earlier, I again had no idea at all what to do. I had missed the wake, when everyone can legitimately turn out to express sympathy, and I simply felt stunned.

I also had my good friends from Tokyo coming to stay the very next day, and we had arranged outings and other activities while they were there, so I was not even on the village site very much until they left. I was delighted that my friends had made the long journey to Kyu-shu, and of course, I needed to find some way to enjoy their company, so I tried to put Sadami's death out of my mind, but it was difficult, and I felt as if a big black cloud was hanging over me. If it had been my own family, everyone would have offered sympathy and leeway, but these were just villagers I didn't even know that well, whereas I had lived with the Tokyo friends for six months on a prior visit. It was during the night that I tossed and turned, even wondering crazy things like whether the four bunches of bananas I had taken for the four children present could be conceived as having caused the sudden death, as the word for 'four' (*shi*) also means 'death' and people avoid it as much as they can.

Eventually I did of course see all the remaining members of the family, and I found a way to express some kind of sympathy. Kiyoka and I did cry together, as it happened. Unsurprisingly she became unwell her-self, and I discovered one day sometime later that the family doctor was treating her for lack of sleep and appetite alongside a general lethargy. She bemoaned the fact that she had not died in her husband's place and almost seemed ready to give up and join him. I urged her to think of the children and asked how they would manage without her, which was a good line, as it turned out, and she rallied a little when I used – probably far too many times – the well-known Japanese expression for hanging in there – *gambatte kudasai* or more informally *gambaranakucha*.

The daughters were to be seen occasionally with other members of the family, and I managed eventually to hand over the photographs I had taken at Tanabata to Atsuko, who seemed briefly cheerful as she looked at them, but generally even the children in the village lost some of their vitality for a while. When a new baby was brought to be presented at the shrine quite soon afterwards, not a single youngster was brought along, and even one of the young relatives hesitated before accepting the rice with red beans which it was customary to hand out to those present. The new mother – for it was her first child – agreed it was probably be-cause people were still in mourning, but she also wondered if she had failed to let people know she was coming to the shrine that day. The Ba-ba family lived near the shrine, but the family of the new baby were from the Western end of the village, which could have been a contributing factor. I did notice that members of more distant houses were less affected by the loss, except perhaps for the schoolfriends of the young daughters.

I had a long conversation with their grandmother, Sadami's mother, who I came across one day doing a job alone outside. I told her that my grandfather, a Christian minister, had been convinced that only very good people die young and she seemed to find some comfort in this idea. She went into detail about how good Sadami had been – to her and to all the family – and I was able to agree that he had also been unusually kind to the stranger who walked into their midst. We didn't exactly hug – it was not a Japanese thing to do at the time – but she certainly went away looking a little less devastated than when I met her, and I was glad to have had the opportunity to give her a little solace in what must have been a terrible bereavement.

I saw the grandfather a few times, carrying out the formalities at the Town Hall, visiting those who had brought condolence gifts, and organising the work that was eventually crying out to be done. He told me in all seriousness that young Sumiko, the eldest daughter, would need to be married off at 16, so that her husband could come and help him take care of the farm. Sumiko was 12, going on 13, at the time, and doing well at school, which would normally be open for her to attend for another 6 years at least, although compulsory for only 3. Even those who married young in Japan at the time were usually in their early 20s, but the law did allow marriage at 16 and this was his solution. Sadly, he didn't let up on this idea and by the time I was next able to go to the village, some 4 years later, Kiyoka and the girls had left for her own family home. Worse still, no one would tell me how to contact her.

In fact, another family had lost a young inheriting son by the time of my next visit, and their solution was reported to have been ideal. This man had been away with friends and had fallen out of a high window when very drunk, so the situation was a bit different, but for the *ie* it was exactly the same. He had three children, all still primary school age, and his parents were still active, but getting older. The wife in this case agreed to take a second husband, who in turn had agreed to move in with a full complement of children and live with his predecessor's parents. It didn't sound too good for him, but life for that household did continue, whereas for the Baba family, it did not, as I will recount in later chapters.

Chapter Seven

Staying Over

HAVING my husband with me to do fieldwork was pleasant for me, although not always for him as I think he tired of living as an adjunct in Japan, despite the attempts of neighbours in our residential community to invite him on various outings. He had also exhausted most of his reading matter, and as this was pre-internet days, he could not access materials online as one could a few years later. He needed to return for the start of the academic year anyway, as he had been offered a research position by his college back in Oxford, which was an opportunity not to be spurned. So, we reluctantly agreed to spend the rest of my year of fieldwork apart, and our beautiful big house became mine alone.

This at first seemed sad, and I have to admit to feeling quite lonely for a while. The only contact I had with my UK friends and family was through letters and a wonderful phone call from my parents at Christmas time, but the decision did turn out to have enormous benefits for the research. There was no language to speak but Japanese, and I had no excuse to return home for my evening meal, so I became free to respond to any, indeed all of the invitations the villagers put my way. I guess they felt a bit sorry for me, and I can't really remember how the practice started, but it became quite common for me to spend nights in the village where I was working, rather than cycling back to my big empty mansion.

This proved fascinating, if a little embarrassing again as I settled into the night time routines of these country people who had befriended me, but it certainly gave me more insight into intimate aspects of home life than my daily visits had managed. Japanese houses are designed rather differently from European ones, and traditionally the main rooms were not strictly divided by function, so that sleeping could take place in a variety of different places within the confines of one home. Beds were being introduced in Japan by this time, and some families had installed them for a new couple, notably if the family of the new bride (or groom in some cases) sent a big double bed along as part of the wedding gifts. However, most farming families were still accustomed to laying out their bedding on the soft *tatami* matting, and it would be rolled up again in the morning to make space for other activities.

Bedding largely consists of *futon*, a name for both the mattress, or mattresses, which are laid out first, and the duvet-like covers which are spread over the top, distinguished with a prefix denoting this purpose. On sunny days these are hung outside to air, and absorb the natural warmth, on dull days they are rolled up and stored in a purpose-built cupboard. In some houses there were also sheets, actually more like enormous towels, spread over the bottom *futon*, and under the top one, possibly because these can be more easily washed than the more perma-nent covers, and another smaller towel might be laid over the pillow in-stalled at one end of the bedding. The towelling material may have been introduced to Japan, and I am not sure why it has become commonplace in bedding except that only small towels are needed after Japan's very hot baths, but there is mention of pillows in ancient Japanese literature, so these are certainly not new. Their stuffing is interesting though, and in the country, it is usually made of buckwheat husks, so quite hard and – for me – a little uncomfortable. This pillow is said to enable a woman to keep her hairstyle intact during the night, and the stuffing also allows air through the husks, so it doesn't get hot and sweaty on steamy summer nights. I suppose I became used to them as there was not really any choice.

The location of my bedding was another interesting aspect of this exercise. There were no 'spare rooms', as we might expect in Western countries, and as I was a guest, I would often be placed in the same room where I had been seated on my first visit, in other words the 'best room' with its decorated 'special' alcove known as a *tokonoma*, and perhaps also the Buddhist altar. However, there seemed to be an idea among my hosts that I would be lonely if I slept by myself, so other members of the family might also lay out their beds there alongside mine. Sleeping together is a common Japanese custom, and friends and family travelling usually also share one big *tatami*-matted room, and indeed, the sleeping area on the ferry Dennis and I had taken from Yokohama (near Tokyo) to Kyushu, consisted of a huge carpeted space where all the economy passengers slumbered side by side.

There was another interesting aspect to this flexibility about sleeping arrangements, by now largely historical, but older people remembered it, and would recount stories they had either been told or had participated in themselves. By the time of my study, it was usual for elders to introduce young people as prospective marriage partners, but only a couple of generations prior to this, young people had been much more active in finding each other. The Youth Group offered opportunities to meet, but a custom known as a 'night creep' (*yobai*) allowed greater commitment to develop. A boy would wrap a towel around his head (a little like those worn for house-building but hiding his identity in this case) and he would steal out of his own home and call round to the home of his chosen girl after most of the older people had settled down for the night. Doors were not usually locked, even when I was there, and the boy would quietly slide back the inner screen to see whether his potential partner was sleeping near enough to the door for a visit. If this worked, the girl would not only be expressing her own willingness to liaise with him, but apparently have convinced her family, if only tacitly, to allow her to cement the relationship in this way. If it didn't work, the boy would return home disappointed, but not usually having been recognised by other night prowlers!

There was only one old lady in the village who actually admitted to having taken part in such an adventure as a preliminary to her eventual marriage, although everyone knew about the custom and would describe variants in an amusing way. The old lady became quite animated in telling her own story, probably because her husband had died a few years earlier and so it was good to share happy memories. Her own family of birth had been one of the paper-makers in the village, and while the process involved several people to create the sheets of paper they were making, she was assigned the last stage, i.e. that of waiting for the last pieces to dry so that they could be taken down and the heaters turned off for the night. Her suitor would come and find her in the paper-making shed, she explained, and there they courted and eventually consummated the love that had been developing between them.

In practice, the last shift in the paper shed was probably a much more private and congenial place for a courtship, in view of the open nature of Japanese houses and way that the rooms are divided only by sliding screens, themselves made of thick sheets of paper, and often with decorative carved wooden panels above them, visible and virtually open to both sides. In fact, privacy was not a quality that was particularly valued in Japan at the time, and rooms with doors were only just being introduced. Dennis and I used to sleep in one of our luxurious 10 rooms, one that happened to open out onto the garden, and one morning, a man who came early to read the electricity meter and found no answer at the front, thought nothing of wandering around to our window to greet us still lying abed at the back, in order to explain his business.

All these aspects of sleeping arrangements in Japan meant that 'staying over' introduced me to family life in a new way, and although people probably adopted some special behaviour to accommodate the visiting foreigner, they did also inevitably reveal to me many of their nighttime routines. The community bath house meant that nothing much was secret, of course, and it was clear with whom I was staying on any one night, as we would turn up together to bathe, and nightly bathing is never something to be skipped in Japan. I had previously timed my own ablutions to coincide with the different age-groups – elderly first, youngsters second, and the housewives last – but I would then cycle off back to my own home whereas now I was able to witness the household routines that explained these distinctions. The young housewives were clearly expected to clear up after the evening meal, which they had probably also made, and this explained their later timing; the men followed a slightly different routine, for the young husbands were not involved in meal preparations so they usually bathed before supper.

They were also quite likely to have meetings and other activities in the evening, and I was able to build up the courage to attend these events as my understanding of the local dialect improved. The political and administrative activities were mostly gatherings of men, but I was encouraged by the families I stayed with to go along, and anyway houses would sometimes send a woman to represent the family as many of these meet-ings were to decide on the duties of houses rather than of individuals. There were also meetings for women. For example, I joined an interesting singing group that met weekly, members taking along quite elaborate tape-recorders in order to bring home and practice the demonstrations of their appointed teacher of songs their own mothers used to sing as they went about their work. These folk songs were apparently becoming less common, I was told, so they needed to be conserved. I also more easily found out about the dates and times of other meetings, so my overall un-derstanding of village life was enhanced tremendously by being invited to stay over.

My memories of walking through the village when I was staying over at night are very positive. There was the aroma of sweet-smelling blossom that seemed to fill the air throughout the seasons, and everyone knew me and greeted me in a friendly fashion. People were relaxed after their days of hard work, and some wandered around draped in little more than a bath towel in the hot summer. They were also much more likely to chat freely than they had been in the daytime, when they were going about their work, and perhaps rushing off to catch the last light. I would also notice what events were taking place simply by being around, and I could pop into the village hall and other venues much more easily than when I had to make a special trip back, close though our house was to the village. I gradually seemed to be becoming a local and it was an incredibly alluring feeling.

Back in the houses where I was staying, there was not often a very long uninterrupted period of sleep. School children working towards ex-ams might be sitting at their desks until the early hours, and young housewives were up before daybreak to get the day's rice under way. In the summer it was common for the elders of the house to be out playing games such as 'gateball', a kind of modification of the English game of croquet, before the sun became too hot, so they would be out of the door at first light. In the winter, it was common for families to huddle together under a big eiderdown spread across a table which sported a heater called a *kotatsu* underneath it, perhaps watching television, and especially chil-dren would simply be allowed to fall asleep in this cosy place. And then, of course, there were men like Sadami, who set off far too early to get their day's work started.

Once the bedding was hung out, or put away, and the *tatami* matting clear, a table could be laid out on the same space for eating break-fast, and in small Japanese apartments, this practice can be quite common. In the country, there are usually more rooms, and they are quite spacious, so a family room with a big table is often set aside for eating and relaxing. If the tatami matting is used, new cushions may be brought out for sitting on the floor, but my country hosts did not necessarily bother with these for themselves, though they sometimes brought one out for me. I had grown used to sitting on the floor in our own house, but they usually knew that foreigners sit on chairs for meals, so they thought I might be uncomfortable. In some houses, the family had installed a table and chairs in the kitchen area, and my neighbours, the Kumagais, were using such an arrangement when I arrived. Funnily enough, they had put the chairs away in a shed by the time I left, proclaiming the floor a preferable place to eat, and relax.

There seemed to be something of a competition to have the for-eigner to stay, and I was for a while inundated with offers of accommo-dation within the village, so I tried to stay with as many families as I could in order not to offend anyone. Of course, I needed to return home to write up my notes, and to keep a record of all the events I was attend-ing, but my house became a haven of peace, rather than a lonely space, and I discovered a new way of proceeding that was very satisfying. I also filled my notebooks with information I would probably never had ac-quired had I not had this opportunity to stay over in the community to which I had become so attached. I think a real turning point in fieldwork arrives when one can almost anticipate the words or actions of the people with whom one is living, and I was for a while lulled into feeling quite confident about this new situation.

Chapter Eight

Living Together

MY complacent life was brought to an abrupt halt one day, however, when I returned to the back door of my own house to find a pair of shoes in the entrance. I used to lock the main front door, the place where we would receive visitors, but the back was used only by myself – and my husband when he had been there – so I was surprised to see that someone else had come inside. Of course, it wasn't my house at all really, it belonged to Mr. Sasabuchi, and at first, I thought he had sent some kind of workman – an electrician, perhaps, or a plumber – as he had been in the habit of sending a gardener to take care of the surroundings from time to time, and maybe he had noticed a problem. I slipped off my own shoes and stepped on in, calling out a greeting to the unexpected visitor.

What followed was alarming to say the least, and I was impressed by my ability to maintain a kind of cool control of which I had no idea I was capable, for as I entered the main room of the house, a man dressed only in a very flimsy nightdress and a pair of knickers, both mine, emerged from the dressing room, and sped for the front door. Like a trapped bird distracted by the glass in a window, he darted from side to side, searching desperately for the lock, and then for the mechanism to release it. 'What on earth are you doing?' I cried, but he ignored me and as he eventually found an escape, I noticed that he had his own clothes tucked under his arm. He ran off to the warehouse at the back, actually a storehouse for the paper supplies of Mr. Sasabuchi, abandoning his shoes, which were, as I mentioned, neatly placed at the back.

I decided the best plan was to call the police, but I felt a little vulnerable in my own now-violated space, so I picked up his shoes and ran around to the office of the Kumagais next door. We called the emergency number, and once Mr. Kumagai had explained that there had been a break-in, I added that if they made haste they would be able to catch the intruder as he had no clothes on when I left him, and indeed, his shoes were in my hands. The response was rapid, indeed Mr. Kumagai and I had hardly had time to walk back to the gate in front of my house, when a police car drew up. The intruder could have made a getaway, as it happened, for his car was at the gate with the engine running, and he was now dressed in his own clothes, but he had gone back to the front door of my house to return my underwear.

Kumagai san recognised the man as an employee of Sasabuchi who came regularly to drop off and pick up paper, and he asked him what he had been doing. The man responded rather quickly. He was supposed to be attending an event at the nursery school of his daughter, so he wasn't expected back immediately, but he had been curious about the foreigner who lived here, and he had gone inside – he made no mention of the change of clothes. Within minutes, the local policeman also arrived on the scene, shook his head vigorously at me, and told me that I should never have let my husband go home. Ah, so the incident was my fault, it seemed, and actually, as I had told few people about my husband's return for just such protection, I wondered how the policeman had found out!

The two men in the original police car were from the city police station, and they had by this time assessed the situation, and asked the intruder to get into their car. Somewhat surprisingly, I thought, they asked me to get in as well, so I went back to secure the house, and did as they asked. It felt slightly uncomfortable to be in the car with this man, but I was in the front and he was in the back, so I suppose that was a separation of sorts. Once we arrived at the police station my intruder was led away so I didn't need to see him again, and I found myself being seated at a table in a large, long room full of uniformed officers.

The questioning which followed took nearly four hours, and as I had been on my way home to get a bite of lunch after a morning's work in the village, one of my overriding memories of the experience was a growing sense of hunger. However, the reaction of the whole of the police station was very interesting, so I slotted into the familiar role of observer, and tried to ignore the pangs. The first problem that took time was that the policemen who were questioning me kept referring to the man who I had found in my house as a burglar. I suppose it was silly of me to argue with them, but I suggested that if he had been a burglar, he could simply have taken the rather expensive camera equipment that had been sitting for all to see on the table and refrained from investigating my clothing.

The suggestion was ignored, and anyway I was a foreigner, so who was I to argue with their use of language, and the interview continued. All the details of my encounter were painstakingly recorded. I can't quite remember why else it took so long, except that perhaps my linguistic abilities were a bit short on legal vocabulary, but one thing I remember very clearly was the last question on their list. This was to ask me what I thought ought to happen to the man now. I must have looked confused, so they persisted. Would you like him to go to prison, they suggested, or to be punished in some other way? I said that I thought the man was probably in need of some psychiatric treatment.

This answer evidently did not find a space any of the boxes they were used to ticking, and they roared with laughter. Actually, not only did they roar with laughter, but they passed my answer on to their curious colleagues sitting at the next table, who in turn passed it on to those on the table beyond, and so on down the room. My answer, which I had thought perfectly appropriate for a man who would enter a house and dress himself in the clothes of its owner, male or female, caused general hilarity throughout the whole police station, and I think I was quite soon to be dismissed.

I have to say that the experience was not a pleasant one, and my main concern was that the man would be locked up, but in fact this was not to be the case. About five days later, the same policemen returned to my house, responded positively to being invited in, and adopted serious expressions on their faces as they arranged themselves around my table. They announced that, after careful consideration, they had decided that the man was not a burglar. Well that was hardly news, but I tried not to gloat. Instead, they described him with a word I did not recognise, so I reached for my dictionary, and found that it translated as 'pervert'. Yes, I nodded, that seemed likely.

Actually, for a long time, I didn't find out what had happened to this man, but meanwhile, my lovely neighbours, the Kumagais, took steps to alleviate my lingering nervousness which not only achieved that aim, but again, made a wonderful contribution to the research. The first interesting thing was the approach. Rather than question my own confidence, Mr. Kumagai came around to say that he was concerned about his own daughters, who were sleeping upstairs by themselves, as he and his wife needed to sleep downstairs with their young boy. Would I consider sleeping upstairs at their house so that I could keep an eye on them, he asked plaintively, mentioning nothing about how this would avoid my own loneliness at home.

We had some further discussion about the practical arrangements, about how I would need to be out working all day, how I would usually take care of my own meals, and how I might sometimes be a little late getting back, but everything was resolved amicably, and I started joining the girls upstairs every night. 'Staying over' became 'living together', and although I was not in the village where I had focused my research, it did lead to a greater understanding of all sorts of unexpected aspects of Japanese life. Staying for odd nights in the village had been wonderful, but odd nights do not reveal much depth in the intimacy of family life, whereas the Kumagais became the close friends whose house has since become my Japanese home whenever I am in the area.

In fact, as I explained earlier, Kiroku had grown up knowing all his age-mates in Kurotsuchi better than the children of his own neighbours in many ways, so I could ask him about their relationships and their history in a way that I felt uncomfortable doing within the village itself. This added to the slight sense of impropriety I felt about interfering in the lives of all these people. As my own son explained to an innocent inquirer many years later, 'anthropologists are just nosey parkers,' but we need to be nosey to find out all about how life works in such different society, and so that is indeed what we do. Somehow life was different with the Kumagais. We had become friends, legitimate friends, and although I was falling deeply in love with Kurotsuchi, the whole village and all its inhabitants, it was an affair I felt I was having rather than a legitimate relationship.

The 'living together' element of my affair had thus become a relationship of a slightly different order, and my legitimate husband had been somewhat usurped by what I came later to think of as truly legitimate friends. This relationship did contribute greatly to my understanding of Japanese social life in general, indeed to family life in particular, but I always slightly resented the fact that Mr. Sasabuchi and Mr. Nishie had not managed to find me a village to study that had an empty house within its boundaries so that the whole process of my research could have taken place within one 'legitimate' context. Over the next few weeks, I spent my nights outside the village of my focus again, so I lost some of the shared neighbourly contact, and although I learned of the internal practices of a Japanese family, almost to the point of embarrassment at times, my acceptance as a local within Kurotsuchi had probably reached its peak before the unanticipated break-in to my own fieldwork residence.

There was another factor contributing to the relationship which ensued, and this is that the family I was now 'living with' were not of quite the same occupational class as the villagers where I was working at that time. The villagers were mostly working in agriculture and horticulture, the rest were craftspeople, making paper, lanterns and bamboo baskets, alongside a couple of carpenters. All perfectly good occupations – I don't want in any way to demean them – but they were of a slightly different order to the paper manufacturer whose father had indeed irked his neighbours only a generation earlier by choosing to enter the industrial classes, an achievement Kiroku Kumagai now shared, though in a lesser way, with our landlord, the much more exalted Sasabuchi *sama*. The Kumagai daughters were studying hard to gain entrance to academic universities, which they both eventually did, and his little son became a doctor, the most highly respected profession in Japan.

Since I came myself from a medical family, I possibly felt more at home with the Kumagais than in the farming village, though I have to reveal that a great part of my personal learning during that year was that absolutely no distinction could be made between the intelligence of the people I was working with based on social class. This was quite a revelation for a product of the still very much class-ridden British system through which I had been born, raised, and educated. My mother, bless her heart, had tried to teach me to dress and behave in a way that suited 'a doctor's daughter', and my father chose to send my brothers and myself to private schools, while we took camping holidays in his native Scotland to help fund them, because he explained quite clearly that 'no one will be able to take your education away from you'. Against all odds, because my girls' school encouraged us to choose caring professions like nursing and secretarial work, I did manage to gain access to university, which I seem to remember in those days was a privilege limited to 2% of the female British population. Mutsuko Kumagai was also the first person to make the journey to Europe after I left. Gradually some of the children of Ku-rotsuchi gained access to academic universities, rather than attend the agricultural college their parents preferred in the interest of continuity, and this of course eventually contributed to the occupational diversity they feared, and which later did indeed emerge.

Meanwhile, however, I continued my research as before, and mounted my bicycle daily to ride over to the village, or sometimes to the city hall where I was still gathering background information. Some inter-esting illustrations of village boundary consciousness emerged during this period, for I was still visiting shops on my own side of the boundary to buy food, and also meeting people from other communities in the process of visiting schools, nurseries, hospitals and other institutions which cov-ered a wider area than the immediate village. One question that often arose was why I had chosen the place of my focus. The people of Kurot-suchi had a reputation of being hard-workers and a local dialect word would pop up regularly: 'they are *gamadashimono*', people would com-ment, almost as a criticism at times, especially after Sadami died so sud-denly. Perhaps Mr. Nishie wanted me to get a good impression of the hard-working Japanese, and that is why he chose a village with such an industrious reputation. Who knows? I certainly don't regret the choice, only the fact that I was staying over the border in another community.

A related factor that emerged was a kind of local loyalty. While I was staying with the Kumagais there was an internal family incident that led to Miyako being hospitalised for three weeks. The details of the inci-dent were explained to me, the grandparents were called in to help out with Atsushi, and the situation was at least partially observed by the employees in the paper factory. I visited Miyako in the hospital and took greetings from those who knew her outside the family. However, although the villagers where I was working knew that she was in hospital, and some asked after her progress when I was amongst them, no one outside the immediate household seemed to know exactly what had happened. They didn't ask me outright to explain, nor did I sense I should offer any further information. I felt a little torn, especially as Kiroku seemed to hold nothing back about the villagers from his own early experience, but I guess anthropologists need also to be diplomatic at times, and this was a prime occasion for such diplomacy.

Chapter Nine

Betrayal

DESPITE the unusual events recounted in the last chapter, my research life continued much as it had always done, with daily visits to the village and the regular writing up of notes, which I was now collecting under headings I had identified as important, notably related to my chosen subject of marriage, but also to village organisation. I spent time down at the town hall too, studying the registration records, a task that became a little tedious as I struggled to read all the difficult Japanese characters people had chosen for their names. Eventually this proved a good exercise, however, as it gave me new reasons to call on all the houses to share the information, and everyone seemed pleased to see the family trees that I was producing for them, to say nothing of the huge village chart that emerged as I brought all the information together. Questions were still emerging, and I carried a notebook specifically to write these down, and then to ask them when a suitable moment occurred.

It was a time of changing moods for me, however, as I missed my family back home, especially as Christmastime drew near, but also as my pleasure and satisfaction working in the village was sometimes shattered with what I regarded – perhaps in vulnerable moments – as complete betrayal. The villagers had, I thought, understood what I was about, that I wanted to participate in as many of their activities as I possibly could, and that I wanted to understand them all in order, when I returned to Oxford, to write a thesis about life in the village and then hopefully a book. All this I had explained everywhere, but in most detail to the head of the village, asking him specifically to let me know when village activities were taking place, and also running with him through the various important activities that were due to take place in the year ahead.

The first time he failed to tell me about an event I was not too upset as I discovered it going on anyway, and the three neighbourhoods each held their own version, so I managed to take part three times, if in different levels of involvement. This event was the festival to celebrate the safe transplanting of the rice seedlings, which I mentioned in Chapters 1 and also Chapter 4, where I explained that it was actually Mrs. Ubiquitous who was keeping me informed about things going on in the village. Each group took time off work to make the straw objects they would hang up beside the streams, and each event was on a different day, as the water for transplanting had to be shared evenly around the community, so I eventually rejoiced on each occasion in being able to spend valuable time with villagers chatting informally amongst themselves.

During the months that followed rice-transplanting, I had been able to build up quite a good idea of how village life was organised, and I had begun to feel that people were cooperating cheerfully with my venture. There had been the summer festival[3] at the main shrine, where the brides and babies were presented to the local deity,[4] and for the festival members of the Youth Group had made sure that I was invited. As also described in Chapter 4, I had watched them work hard to plait a new straw *shimenawa* to hang at the entrance[5] and I had witnessed the visit of the Shinto priest[6] to prepare paper streamers to shake over the officials whose duty it was to carry out the rituals. I had been able to observe and photograph all aspects of the procedure, including the part of the occasion to hand over the duty to another neighbourhood for the festival next year.

It struck me particularly hard then one day to find that I had been completely missed out of a second crucial village festival, which involved a rather similar procedure, but this time at the *Shinboku* – the tree sacred to the God of Thunder and Lightning – that was in a less obvious location, down a path between two houses. This shrine[7] was clearly important to the village, for the baseball players had chosen the English name 'Flashers' for their team, having no idea of the less than charming

---

[3] See illustration on page 3.
[4] See illustrations on pages 30 and 31.
[5] See illustration on page 29.
[6] Illustration on page 32 shows a similar Shinto priest.
[7] See illustration on page 5.

meaning of the English word, but knowing only that it approximately translated the Japanese term for thunder and 'lightening' (*kaminari*) – and the destructive flash of lightning that had felled the original tree at the site. It was that sacred tree that gave the village an identity different to all the others, which always have a general shrine for the local god who takes care of the villagers.

The festival and handover at the tree happened in September, when I was preparing to send Dennis off back to the UK, and I only discovered a couple of days later that it had taken place when I noticed a new *shimenawa* had been hung, festooned with newly crafted paper streamers. To say I was upset would be an understatement, for I felt totally let down. This was a once-a-year event, so the only chance I would have to see it, and it was probably the most sacred spot in the village. Had they perhaps deliberately excluded me, I wondered? There was no intrinsic reason why the villagers should respond to my request to attend all their events, indeed they would be quite within their rights to be relieved that the foreigner was not always there, but I could not help feeling quite devastated. I had begun to feel part of the community, I had almost relaxed in the knowledge that they enjoyed having me around, but no one had thought to let me know about this important occasion.

I strode angrily off to the house of the head of the village, the man who had been kind enough to invite me us to his son's wedding when Dennis and I first arrived in the area, and I undoubtedly made clear my disappointment, for he began immediately to tell me about other activities that were coming up, and that I would be welcome to attend. This man was in fact a prime example of a good diplomat, because he was initially able to diffuse my ire, but he was clearly not to be trusted on all fronts. This was also the man who had looked coyly at his wife when I had first explained that I was interested in comparing love and arranged marriages, and he had double-checked that love marriages were the norm where I came from (in those days, usually referred to as 'over there'), as if implying that they had themselves been an early example of the charming foreign practice. During my stay I discovered that he had refused to allow his own daughter to marry someone with whom she had proclaimed to be in love, and I had later overheard him sharing his doubts about such unions to a group of fellow older men.

The good news about his daughter was that she managed to find a benevolent uncle to approach her father, and in his presence to introduce her to her proposed partner as if they had never met before. This introduction, known as a *miai*, was the customary way of arranging a union at the time, and her father had graciously agreed, so everyone was happy in the end. Clearly the daughter had inherited some of her father's diplomatic skills, and the conclusion I took home from his initial suggestion of a love union with his own wife, was that I needed to be careful of the Japanese tendency to appear positive about the customary practices of others even if they do not agree with them. The head of the village revealed another continuing misunderstanding as I was leaving on the occasion of my complaints about betrayal for he asked again, in all seriousness, whether it was really me, and not Dennis, my husband and a man who had only ever entered the village in order to attend his son's wedding, who was carrying out the research for a doctorate at Oxford University.

On this subject of gender, and a general hierarchy also based on age, another interesting aspect of my attendance at village gatherings, when it was allowed, was where they chose to place me. The seating order at local events was quite strict. Hosts would place guests at the top – seats in front of the central house post, usually found beside the *tokonoma* special place described in Chapter 7 – and other attendees would arrange themselves in age order towards the bottom, men above women. Now, I never did quite understand why they chose this position for me, but I was always automatically placed in the middle, above the women and below the men. It meant I could listen and ask questions in both directions, so I didn't complain, but I was slightly worried that a young woman being placed above my elders might be perceived badly. With time and experience in Japan, I realised that whatever a foreigner does is usually fine, however much we worry about getting things right, so it was as well to relax!

So, was I being betrayed when people failed to tell me about events? Had I any right at all to expect my odd situation to be understood by the villagers who had had no choice at all in having me in their midst (as far as I know)? Throughout my stay, I was often nervous about imposing on peoples' lives, but I needed to complete the task on which I had embarked so I pressed on – and indeed, as I have already explained somewhat out of chronological order in Chapter 7, many people did invite me to stay over with them after Dennis left, so I should certainly not have felt neglected. One thing that I did learn during my research was that people were often as curious about me as I was about them so, as at that very first wedding, if I was willing to answer their questions, they would happily answer mine. And what fuels the research of an anthropologist but curiosity, so at least we all had that in common about each other, though I could probably have done without the curiosity of the man who wanted to try on my underwear!

I did have another sort of company back at the beautiful home we had been lent for the period of my visit, for not long after Dennis and I took up residence, we noticed that there was a dog living underneath the building. I don't know whether it was there when we arrived, but we noticed it quite soon afterwards, and Dennis, in his usual habit of assigning nicknames to everyone, decided to call it Dave. In fact, this turned out to be a misnomer, because Dave eventually produced a litter of puppies, but the name stuck, and we didn't bother to change it on finding Dave had become a mother. I did ask a few people in the neighbourhood if they had lost a dog, but most laughed and shook their heads, explaining that he would be a stray (*norainu* – literally 'come from the wild'). Probably not a strict definition, because people in Japan whose pets have puppies they don't want usually leave them in a box outside somewhere, rather than disposing of them by drowning, or chloroform, both methods used in Western countries, so wandering dogs were not unusual.

Dave didn't bother us much, and I did occasionally throw edible left overs out for him, or her, and her offspring, but after I returned from Tokyo when I went to see Dennis off and check in with my supervisor there, she did run up happily to see me, wagging her funny little short tail in delight. What could I do? I grew up with dogs and I was pleased to have at least an animal for company, so I continued to throw over the odd delicacy – though I decided not to make them too regular so that she would not become too dependent on someone who was definitely set to leave in due course. My attempted cooling-off manoeuvre didn't really work, however, because she began to run along beside my bicycle when I went out, and her presence disturbed some of the people I was visiting, so Dave became a bit of a problem, as well as company!

Two further problems emerged through my harbouring of stray animals under the house. One was when Dave went into heat again, and a series of young suitors began to lurk about the premises. I tried to chase them away, especially when the old faithful father of the first litter of puppies appeared one day all tattie and beaten up, with blood around one of his eyes. My efforts were not entirely successful in that matter either for it was not long afterwards, when I was down at the local post office, that they informed me that the postman would no longer be able to deliver to my house because of the large number of dogs he was encountering there. I tried to persuade them that the dogs were benign, but soon decided that I had better not push the matter in case the poor delivery man did get bitten and the fault would be mine. They agreed to leave my post with the Kumagais and, as I was staying there anyway by this time, it was not really a problem.

The second incident did leave me feeling very bad, however. One evening, as the autumn began to draw in, and the weather became a little chilly, a kind local couple came to the door to ask me if I would like to borrow a *kotatsu*. This is the rather ingenious Japanese device that has not really spread too far around the world that I described in Chapter 7, a table with a heater underneath it, used with a large eiderdown spread over the top so that one can snuggle down and keep warm while sitting at it. Preferably wearing a padded jacket to keep the back warm! Well, of course, I said yes, how kind, and I invited them in for a cup of coffee.

We chatted for a while, and when they took their leave, we went to the door and found that one each of their tidily placed pairs of shoes had disappeared. Sadly, they had left the outside door open behind them as they came up into the house, and clearly the dogs – or perhaps the puppies – had found the shoes and carried them away. I quickly took a torch and spent some time hunting around for them, but despite my best efforts, I found only one shoe, that of the husband, and it was chewed quite badly around the back. I guess the shoes of my kind visitors were made of leather, or something tastier to puppies than my own trainers, for they had completely ignored mine. I offered to replace them, of course, but they steadfastly refused, and I felt bad every time I snuggled down under the *kotatsu* – I didn't even know these people very well, and they had been so kind – perhaps I stopped thinking about betrayal at that point.

Chapter Ten

First Break-Up

THE last few weeks of my work in Yame raced by in a frenzy of activity, the pages of my diary becoming less and less coherent as the completion of named notebooks became a priority, and I tried to balance invitations with ensuring I had all the information I needed to start on my thesis when I got back to the university. The period was anyway a busy one, as New Year approached, and this is a time when much celebration takes place all over Japan. The villagers were not a problem; indeed, I was delighted by the events they were organising, especially as some of them were for my benefit. However, quite suddenly, representatives of various groups from the wider city of Yame rushed around to invite me to end-of-year parties, which I could hardly refuse as they had always been pretty helpful, but these were not really much use, or even fun, for me. The Rotary Club was excruciating, for they asked me to give a 10-minute talk, which was nerve-wracking enough, and then their sister club in nearby Kurume, asked me to do it all over again! A local radio station decided it wanted to broadcast an interview with me, and again, a repeat performance was requested.

I suppose all this activity took my mind off the fact that Christmas was passing almost unnoticed, except for the consumption of a large number of sickly cream cakes, which had been chosen generally in Japan to mark the occasion. There were also visits for small children from Santa Claus, a commercial venture arranged by department stores selling toys, and Atsushi received such a visit. The Kumagais did cook a special meal, which was nice, and my parents sent me a tape of lovely music, and timed in a short, but very expensive phone call, which was a wonderful present. It is difficult with the amazing advances in technology since those days to remember that our only communication except for that one call were the weekly letters we wrote to each other, and I was now always awaiting the less frequent ones from Dennis. Being left to handle my affair alone became less exciting as it drew to an inevitable break-up.

I rushed around trying to complete various tasks I had set myself to do before I left, and a notable one was a visit to a local faith healer. He called himself a 'high priest of Buddhist faith' although he seemed to have no official connection to the more recognisable Buddhist temples in the district. He had a long grey beard and wore white robes. I was taken by a woman who was worried about her sick husband, and the priest claimed that he could travel in spirit form to enter the body of the man lying at home, diagnose the disease, and return with advice for his visitor. For this purpose, he sat at his Buddhist altar and chanted rhythmically and repeatedly, seemingly putting himself into a kind of trance. We waited politely, and after a while he came back to talk us through his experience, the treatment he had already administered, and to give my companion recommendations about how to continue to look after her husband.

I am not sure whether this woman had also consulted a doctor, but other people spoke of the multiple ways in which they attempted to treat themselves or relatives when they were unwell. They certainly might visit a hospital or go and see a Western-trained doctor, but in Japan there are also specialists in Chinese medicine, and shops that sell Chinese medicines over the counter, and these are well used too. Many people would go to shrines to pray for their recovery, and of course, others beside my companion above would call on a variety of faith healers and diviners. I took my own son to such a healer on one occasion, and he recovered despite a hospital failing to heal his stomach upset – but I jump ahead – he wasn't born yet! The same specialists are consulted about the suitability of marriage partners, apparently, and one girl I met had changed the Chinese characters she used to write her name because she had been advised by such a person that this would be more auspicious.

As the end of the year approached, many household decorations appeared, which were also said to seek good fortune, this time for the year ahead. They were hung on doors, laid out on shelves, and even attached to the front of cars, tractors and other work machinery. Ferns for prosperity, a vine leaf for health, and *mikan* oranges were used within the house, the last a variety called *daidai mikan* because *daidai* also means generations and symbolises that these should continue through time. Pine, bamboo and plum provided the background to some of the decorations, as in betrothal gifts, symbolising persistence and strength in adversity, as pine trees thrive in the most precarious positions, resilience, as bamboo plants bend and retract in the strongest of winds, and plum because it is the first blossom to appear in the early spring and can survive lingering snow and frosts. It is said to symbolise hope for the year ahead.

New Year household decoration

Everyone around me was busy tidying up their outstanding tasks for the end of the year and preparing for the mandatory three-day holiday that would come on the morning of January 1st when no one is supposed to work, not even housewives, so special long-lasting rice cakes called *mochi* are made. At midnight at the end of the year, Buddhist temples ring their bells 108 times, to get rid of the 108 human sins according to a Buddhist view. Families travel all over Japan to be with their relatives, and I had a visit from the daughter of a neighbour of my mother in England who had been studying Japanese, so the two of us were invited to join people in Kurotsuchi to take part in various celebrations. Yasuro also came to visit again, but he took off on the 31st to spend the actual transfer of years with his parents in nearby Saga. Yasuro's mother was the one who helped me equip my kitchen when we first arrived, so I needed to make a visit to see her too, and eventually to return the things she had lent me.

On January 1st we went around greeting people, and two families took us off up nearby hills to visit shrines at the top to pray for a good year. Otherwise we were invited into people's homes to share the special food they had prepared, and to meet the visiting relatives, sometimes those I had met back in the summer when *Obon* was being celebrated.

Obon was a celebration for the ancestors, and to remember the things they did in the past; New Year on the other hand, is more oriented towards the future, to make a new start, and pray for good things to come. At *Obon*, lanterns had been set up to remember those who had died during the past year, at New Year, special gifts were displayed in the *tokonoma* in houses where babies had been born. We also all visited a big local shrine in Yame on January 3rd, where talismans bought the previous year were burned, and new ones purchased to ensure protection for the coming year.

The passage into the New Year is also when people officially clock up one year in age, and young people who had become 20 began to prepare to take part in a special ceremony on January 15th to mark their entry into adulthood. Girls usually wear kimono, and boys, smart suits, or Japanese garments called *hakama haori*, and they are reminded by city officials at the town hall of their new status and the duties now incumbent upon them. Members of the youth group in Kurotsuchi held a more informal party for the members who had achieved this status, and they invited me to join them. As it was drawing close to the time I would leave, they made it an occasion also to wish me well. One of the advantages of becoming an adult in Japan is that it is now legal to consume alcohol, so those who achieved that status were regaled with a variety of drinks, as well as being given presents, and although we also ate big plates of *sukiyaki*, the occasion became quite drunken. I left at around 10.30 pm, but I believe celebrations continued for some time afterwards!

The villagers in fact gave me an amazing send-off one way and another. Once I let people know the date of my departure, many people came round with gifts. Sometimes these were things which in Japan can be passed on to others without any sense of guilt and I had a few debts to repay, notably in the community where Dennis had made friends, and I had also been treated well, so some of these were simply reassigned. It is just the way that these things work in Japan, and many people keep a cupboard for gifts received that can later be passed on. Others brought me cash – 'for the journey' – and I soon learned of the custom of sending away people travelling with money for the purchase of gifts to be brought back to those very same donors! Fortunately, I made a detailed list of who had brought me what, but it did worry me for quite a long time just how I was going to bring back enough gifts from 'over there', as many perceived my destination, to satisfy a whole village. This was just the beginning of said worry, incidentally... but I jump ahead again.

I had taken a trunk to Japan with me, and it was not dispatched until shortly before I left, so I could manage to accommodate many of the gifts I was given, but one present that was delivered just as Dennis was departing had proved quite problematic. It was an example of a local craft, namely a lantern made from the lava that lies around the volcanoes that have erupted in the area in the past, and it was large, heavy, and simply impossible for him to carry to the airport. We explained our di-lemma, and asked the kind donors, whom we hardly knew I have to say, if they could send it to Dennis back in Liverpool, where his family was located. I wrote out his parents' address and off they went. Actually, the lantern did eventually occupy a nice spot in our garden in Oxford, but not before my poor father-in-law, who did not drive, had to arrange to pay quite a large sum of import duty, and to have the box picked up from the port and taken to their house in Liverpool while Dennis found us a home in Oxford. Dennis was their only son, and thoroughly spoiled, so I guess they didn't mind too much!

Before I departed, the housewives in Kurotsuchi organised a wonderful send-off party for me in the village hall, and we gathered and shared memories, made promises to visit again in the fu-ture, and gobbled up some tasty good-ies. I did invite everyone to come and visit me too, of course, quietly praying that it would be a few years before a village group would arrive in Oxford. The present the housewives had assem-bled for me was a *hagoita*, a 'badminton racquet' or 'battledore' that historically would be used in a game so it did come accompanied by a small feathered shut-

The *hagoita* presented to me when I left the village in 1976

Photograph taken with the village housewives in 1976

tlecock, but it was decorated with a beautiful Japanese doll, dressed in a fine silk kimono, and with an elaborate hairstyle, held in place with a series of pins, so I didn't plan on waving it about too much. These are the same objects given to baby girls in Japan at New Year to wish them good fortune, and subsequently displayed in the *tokonoma*, but mine had a wonderful surprise on the back. It had been signed by every woman in the village, so made a splendid souvenir, which I could carry home.

A photograph was taken of the assembled company, and as I discovered on my next and subsequent visits, was from then on displayed in the village hall! A send-off party was also organised for the children's group, and this took place on the afternoon of the ceremony for young adults, so everyone was still on holiday. Another lovely photograph was taken, and my actually rather ephemeral presence in the community was again recorded for posterity. Meanwhile, I packed and prepared to leave. I sent the trunk on ahead, but I needed to guard carefully all my notes and my own photographs. In those days my notes were handwritten, and copying was not yet an easy task, so I worried about keeping them safely, and likewise, the photographs I had taken often only existed in single copies. Some were black and white, and these had negatives, and I had made copies to give out as gifts, but the colour slides were one-offs and very precious, so they also need to be carried with care.

On the day that I actually departed for the UK, I took a train from the station that was literally a few steps from our borrowed house, and

Party to see me off at the local station when I left in 1976

there was quite a gathering on the tiny platform to see me off. This time it was mostly the men from Kurotsuchi who came – the younger ones – but the Kumagais were out in full force. Again, photographs were taken, and one of my overriding memories was the sad faces of the girls with whom I had shared a bedroom, and the little two-year-old boy who could not hold back his tears. He held out his little arms for me to hug him farewell and carried on holding them out sadly as I boarded the train. I was heading home to my legitimate lover, and looking forward to seeing my family, but it was quite a wrench to leave the community with which I had conducted such an intimate affair. It was not really a break-up as I assured them that I would return, and addresses had been exchanged, but I could give no definite date, and Oxford was a long way away.

Chapter Eleven

A Glorious Return

A FTER I left Kurotsuchi the first time, I had of course to return to Oxford to write my thesis, and there was a period of separation from that life in Japan, although I thought about it daily and contemplated everything in more detail than I had ever managed when I was there. It took a while to separate my emotional involvement from the expected academic work, and my first submission to my supervisor was possibly too romantic sounding. It simply described the area and the activities of the people I had worked with, as anthropological accounts are wont to do, but I clearly failed to hit the mark, for the reaction of my supervisor was cutting:

'Shall I put this in the bin, or will you?'

Nice one!

The thesis did eventually get written, and it passed muster eventually as well. It took some time, however, because I decided that while I was pretty much confined to writing at my desk, I might as well also think about starting a family. This plan did interfere slightly with my ability to write up the thesis at speed, because my first son was conceived almost as soon as we let nature take its course, and I had promised Dennis, also settling in to his own thesis writing, that I would take care of everything at home if we were to have a child immediately. I thus became a doctoral-student-housewife, which in fact worked out quite well because my literal 'confinement' was relatively trouble-free, and young James, when he arrived, was an easy baby to work around. In later years, my students would shake their heads in frustration that they didn't have the same success, so I guess I was lucky.

We had moved into a charming village in the country by the time I gave birth, where we rented a 16th century stone cottage, so I had plenty of nice photographs to send back to my friends in Japan who had anyway never stopped asking when we would be making our children. In those days, there was no social media of course, and letters were the main means of keeping in touch. I couldn't really write to all the villagers, so communication was a bit sporadic, but I had left my address in the village and I did receive several letters, usually from grandmothers who had time to write. They had completed six years of schooling so could manage quite beautiful Japanese script, which looked charming, but I sometimes found it difficult to decipher completely. Some characters have been simplified since their schooling, and they were also prone to choosing the wrong characters at times – ones that had the pronunciation they were after, but not the meaning – so I sometimes needed to consult Japanese friends living in Oxford to get the full significance of their missives... but it was wonderful to keep in touch, and I made a point of writing back to those who wrote to me.

Once I had finished writing the thesis, which was submitted in 1979, I began to think about publishing it, and an interesting encounter brought not only a publisher, but a return trip to the village. The BBC Education channel was making a series of programmes about Japan at the time and they were looking for someone who had worked in a village to introduce them to rural life. Friends at the Japanese Studies Department at Sheffield University put the producer in touch with me, and once she heard about my fieldwork, she invited me to travel back to Japan for a month to prepare the villagers for filming and to act as an interpreter during the process. Of course, I needed to get permission from the people who would be filmed and arrange for the care of my young son, but as it turned out, the villagers were delighted, my parents and parents-in-law readily sketched out cover for my absence, and plans were made for a new trip. The icing on the cake – or at least it seemed so at the time – was that the brother of the BBC producer happened to be a publisher, and he actually approached me about publishing my thesis!

It was mid-afternoon when I arrived back in Yame. A strangely quiet time when few people are about to notice the renewed presence of a familiar but unmistakably foreign face. The older children were still not home from school, and my previous neighbours, though evidently pleased to see me, were unable, with only a small shy son who did not at first remember me, to orchestrate the welcome I had fondly imagined. However, as we began to talk and exchange news, the odd nagging fears I had had about this return were gradually and warmly dispelled.

'We'd like to have you stay with us the whole time you are here', Mr. Kumagai said, 'but when you get to the village, you'll find they have organised a rota of families to accommodate you. I doubt you'll be able to turn them down'.

I had no intention of turning them down; in fact, I was delighted to hear that they had been so concerned. It is not easy to be sure of one's relationship with a village. With families, perhaps, with individuals more surely, but with a village – it is quite difficult! This was a testing time, and the rota of accommodation seemed an extremely good omen. As conversation with the Kumagais reached a lull, I decided it was time to advise the village head of my arrival. Omens are picturesque, but I was here to work, and the success of the venture depended to a great extent on the goodwill and cooperation of the villagers.

I thought of walking over there, but the Kumagais offered me a bike, so I cycled, just as I had always done. I was surprised to find that I almost missed the turn off the main road, but once in the village, it was as if time had failed to pass. The old headman's plot was as neat as ever, and his vegetables looked healthy, as they had always been. At first sight, little seemed to have changed and I had to remind myself that over three years had passed since I had last cycled over there. I didn't even know for sure who the headman would be, so I went to the old headman's house to find out. No one responded to my call at the door, but I soon found his married son in a greenhouse not far away. He smiled to see me but seemed slightly tongue-tied. He seemed so unchanged, and his circumstances and attitude so much as I had always found them, that I felt quite strange going through the greetings usual after a long separation. This feeling recurred with almost every new meeting. Everything was so familiar; the faces I had feared I might not recognise were so well known to me. Yet I also often felt I was too quick to get down to business, that I should have spent more time in nostalgic chatter.

The new headman was the person I had expected, even feared slightly, for in his previous role as village treasurer he had always seemed efficient almost to the point of brusqueness, sometimes a little impatient with my continual and probably naïve sounding questions. However, he was effusive in his welcome and evidently well prepared from my letter to cooperate in every way he could. I was surprised and flattered to find that a welcome party had been planned for myself and the film crew, not only by the village, but also to include the mayor and several other city dignitaries. As Mr. Kumagai had anticipated, he was anxious that I should move into the village and take up the hospitality arranged by the Housewives' Association. Before I could leave, and despite protests that I was expected for supper, a tray was placed before me that I felt it would be offensive to refuse. Shortly after my solitary meal, I returned for a feast prepared in my honour back at Kumagais. Thus, I began again to build up obligations I seemed never able to repay, to incur kindness and concern on a scale that it is difficult even properly to describe.

The following day I moved to the first house on the list. It was a family to which I had always been particularly attracted, the family which I had seen suffer a grief so grave I could only imagine its magnitude, and I had kept in touch through an infrequent, though regular exchange of rather polite letters. It was the family with whom I had rather hoped to stay but feared to ask directly since I was unsure of their states of health, especially as I had heard that the daughter-in-law and three granddaughters had moved out. It was the family with whom in the end I spent my entire time during that visit. They treated me like a daughter, a long-lost one who is thereby accorded special treatment and attention for a while, and no one seemed to mind too much that I did not move around the village, according to the previous plan. This family's name was Baba, introduced in Chapter 6.

That same second day, the head of the village took me up to the tea fields to see the hand-picking of the first harvest. Just as I remembered the smooth cylindrical bushes covered the whole of the visible hillside, in neat parallel lines, tidily divided into plots, here and there bedecked with a colourful team of pickers working steadily, gracefully along the rows. Before I had settled on a place to do my year of 'fieldwork', it had been this sight which had finally tipped the balance of indecision in favour of my choosing this particular village. It was so well organised, so clearly laid out, evidently so efficient and profitable. It was very Japanese.

I met again a number of the people I had known so well, with whom I had worked at the same task four years previously.[8] It seemed appropriate that I should start this second, albeit much shorter stay at the same time of year, in the same setting, with the same atmosphere. Four years before I had found the tea fields a good focus for my attention during the first few weeks, a convenient place to meet people when I was still rather shy of calling at houses, an orderly place from which to start the analysis of a confusion of impressions. It was also a good place to raise the idea of a BBC crew coming to film them, and they agreed quite readily. My work was begun.

During the next few days, I drew up a list of planned village events so that we could make a timetable for the filming once the four-man crew arrived. I found that the city dignitaries had booked a hotel for their foreign guests, who had made their own plans to hire a car on arrival, so practical details were underway. I should perhaps remind readers that Dennis and I had been the only European residents in Yame up to that point, with so few temporary visitors that the hosts of one unsuspecting foreigner who turned up had called me to enable us to speak to each other! The film crew was thus given a right royal welcome, and they did their best to comply with local expectations, which I sometimes had to explain to them, but they were all used to working abroad and for the most part caused no offence.

During the three week visit, we filmed all the daily activities, the usual work of the village: tea picking, chrysanthemum house maintenance, rice planting, and the wonderful *kawa matsuri*; we found shrine cleaning and road surface mending to record, as well as sports and dancing beside the shrine at the sacred tree, and singing practice in the village hall. The children walking home from school made excellent footage, as did a man shooing his geese along the road and into the stream. The cameraman made detailed recordings of crafts such as papermaking and bamboo work, as well as creating the beautiful lanterns that stand beside the Buddhist altar when someone has died. They filmed the monthly exercise to check the local fire engine was working, and then, as if on cue, a real

---

[8] See illustration on page 6.

A bride with the shrine maiden and go-between

fire broke out the next day in an adjacent community, and we managed to find them a back-way round to film the professionals in action as well.

We interviewed the head man and various elders of the village about the way life worked in this community, which the BBC producer presented as a model for social life in the other 14 films he made for the educational series he called *Inside Japan*, and later, when we all returned to the UK, I was tasked with translating it all for a voice-over! Two other exciting events that happened while we were there was a house-building, with all the neighbours out to help, just as I had witnessed and described in my thesis,[9] and the wedding of the middle sister of the paper-making family, which became a prime feature of the film. The wedding itself was splendid, as usual, but there were also colourful preparations, like the delivery of the betrothal gifts[10] and the sending off of the bride's trousseau.

I was relieved throughout to find that everyone seemed delighted to take part, the head of the village proud to show off their multitude of organised activities, and all the participants most professional in the way they carried them out before the rolling camera. There was one deeply embarrassing morning, when the crew

Bride and groom share cups of *sake*

[9] See illustration on page 31.
[10] See illustration on page 27.

86

turned up complaining bitterly for some field preparatory work that I had been told would take place at 6 a.m., only to find it was all over – they had moved it forward to 5 a.m. without letting me know. That stung, and created some bad feeling for a while, but at the end of the designated filming period, the villagers threw a wonderful party, out in the open air beside the sacred tree, and we ate and drank together in a relaxed, happy fashion before we all took off in our different directions to make our way home.

My visit had been short, and it sped by in a flurry of organisational manoeuvres and incessant translational demands, but I felt that we had accomplished what we set out to do, and I left promising that the villagers would receive their own copy of the resulting film as soon as it was ready. Sadly, there was little time to go over things, but because I had readily shown everyone pictures of the two-year-old son I had left behind, I was swamped with presents to take home for him. My existing suitcase could not accommodate even half of them, and I was packed off to the airport with a couple of large bags marked clearly as for the use of members of the agricultural union! Fortunately, the check-in desk was sympathetic, and they bundled everything into a more substantial box, and dispatched it to London.

Chapter Twelve

Infidelity?

FILMING with the BBC had been an exciting experience for me and for the villagers, and I suppose I went home on a high, so pleased was I that everything seemed to have gone well. I was also happy to be reunited with my son James, who was after all only two-and-a-half years old. I had been warned that he might spurn me at first for leaving him for almost a month, but he ran happily up the path to greet me when I arrived, and my parents and parents-in-law seemed to have enjoyed their visits. The health visitor had called while I was away and some department of the local Council summoned me when I got back, which was a little alarming, but I guess I was glad they cared enough about my son's welfare to check on my mother's reassurance that all was well! Apart from that, I was a little overwhelmed with the large number of presents I was carrying. I had worked hard to take back appropriate gifts for those in Japan who had sent me off with money and objects to carry home, but now I felt quite overloaded with a new set of obligations.

Still, we had made a good film, I was delighted when I saw it, and we arranged to send a copy of it to Japan so that the villagers could share it too. Interviews had been translated into English, but at least they would have the images to look at, and people would see themselves going about their daily lives. I also responded positively to the idea raised by the brother of the producer of the film to publish my thesis with his company, and I submitted it more or less as it was for consideration. It received some critical reviews, but the publisher went ahead anyway, simply using the criticism as an excuse to take out the photographs I had prepared. Over the years I have regretted being so speedy about getting into print because I think there could have been two books, one about marriage, the subject mentioned in the title, and another about the village, in each case responding to the anonymous readers' suggestions, but I was keen to see my work in print, and I concurred.

It would be another 2 years before I encountered the real reactions of my stars to the film and saw the polite disappointment on their faces when I handed over copies of a book they couldn't read. Meanwhile, I gave birth to my second son, William, and I was also offered a half-time job at Oxford Polytechnic, so I became quite busy back in Oxford. I probably neglected to write back quite so often to my correspondents in Kurotsuchi, though I did send them photographs of my expanding family, but it was another piece of unexpected good fortune for us that became the third example of something I began in retrospect to feel was a kind of infidelity in my love affair with Kurotsuchi.

I had kept in touch with Takako, my oldest Japanese friend in Tokyo, and we had both become mothers of small children, so in a flurry of excitement about my burgeoning career as a social anthropologist, I applied for a grant from the London office of the Japan Foundation, a Japanese organisation supporting research in Japan, to return with my children to do some comparative work on the subject of pre-school child care. Takako and I had discussed how we might manage this, and she persuaded the head of the kindergarten attended by her daughter not only to help with the project and offer James a place there, but to lend us a staff house that was standing empty beside it in which we could live for six months. The headmistress herself had a beautiful house in the same grounds, so we would become part of a new community in Japan, situated in a seaside town some 800 miles from Yame. We received the grant, which was generous enough to enable me to take our doctor's daughter to help me with the domestic tasks, and my second research trip was underway.

I had of course factored in a trip to Yame, as I knew everyone would want to meet the children, and Dennis was able to take enough time off work to come with us for that part of the visit, so as the summer holidays began, Dennis flew in and we made our way to the ferry terminal. Just as we had done for our first trip to Kyushu, we spent two nights on board, but this time we took a cabin, so we had a bit more privacy than the shared carpet had provided on our first journey from Yokohama to Kyushu. It was exciting for the children, who were four years and a mere 17 months at that stage, and they were of course over the moon to see their Dad, but almost as soon as Dennis arrived, I had the impression that he was there under sufferance. He had brought several books to read and each time he started a new one, he listed the days of his visit that remained, and ticked them off rather obviously every morning.

At first, our arrival in the village was also exciting. We spent a few days with the Kumagais, who were all still resident in the house that had been our neighbour, and were delighted to see Dennis again, and meet our children. Then we looked after their house, as it was the summer festival of *Obon* and they went off to visit the Hiroshima grandmother, and asked me to take care of the *miso* bean paste, which needed turning over twice a day. Then later, we moved in *en masse* with the Baba family, actually only the grandparents by that time, but they had invited us to a big gathering at *Obon* with the two younger sons who had set up home elsewhere, but brought their wives and children over to remember the brother they had lost, and their own grandparents. James and Will were thoroughly spoilt there, but I think Granny Baba[11] was happy to have them, and we did feel very welcome. So, there was no problem with our hosts.

We also set up a time to show the film in the village hall, but what gradually emerged as I made my way around the houses was that many people were disappointed because they knew they had been filmed, but they had not appeared in the final version. I guess this is inevitable when a film crew comes to town. In this case, the crew had shot eleven hours of footage, and the film was only 50 minutes long, so any one scene had less than a 10 percent chance of being part of it. Worse still, the family that had featured most because their daughter happened to be getting married, had experienced discrimination from the other families that felt hard done by because their own contribution had been more or less ignored. So, I did feel that, somehow, I had let many people down.

As for the book, which was now out and available, I did take a few copies with me. I gave one to my hosts, one to the head of the village,

[11] Granny Baba appears on the bottom-right of the photograph of the village housewives which appears on page 78.

James catching crayfish with a friend in Kurotsuchi

and one to Hideshi's family because he and his wife were the wedding couple who appeared on the front cover – they were one of several who got married during my fieldwork, but it was the best photograph. Unfortunately, the family that was featured in the film was also the main house of the family whose son's wedding photograph was depicted on the front of the book – the grandfathers were brothers – so I guess that may have caused some trouble too. More disappointing about the book, however, was that there were no other photographs, despite my submission to the publisher, and none of them could read it.

Later, when I was back in Oxford, I received a letter one day asking permission to have a translation made. The head of the village had found a translator, but they needed my permission. I was slightly nervous, because a bad translation could be worse than no translation at all, and I asked Professor Matsunaga if he would take a look at the pages they had already had done. He agreed, but deemed it a very bad effort, and when I discovered that the sections I had translated literally from the Japanese into English had been put back into very different Japanese, despite my provision of the source of the originals, I found myself in agreement with him. Sadly, I withheld my permission, but of course, I have no idea whether they went ahead.

During our three-

William playing with the granddads at the shrine

week stay in the village that time, the children charmed everyone, James because he was fluent and funny in Japanese after attending kindergarten for a few months, and William probably just for being a blond baby, whom everyone in Japan seemed to find 'cute' (*kawaii*). Even Granny Baba, who must have found them a bit of a trial filling her quiet house, indulged them horribly, and overall, we detected no further bad feeling. Other young mothers in the village seemed happy to share their ideas about child rearing, and I was eventually able to add a comparative section about rural methods to the book I wrote on that subject. This time there were photographs, and the front cover featured the children of the couple who had appeared on the first one but playing in the shrine compound with their grandfather. I don't know if anyone cared about that choice, I never heard any more about it. For me, it looked a little old-fashioned as children in the cities were more likely to attend a nursery than to have the clearly close attentions of a grandparent, but again, the picture was chosen by the publisher, and it was a good one.

My next two visits to Kurotsuchi were also made as part of a wider project, and they were not very long, but it was good to keep in touch with people, to visit the Buddhist altars of houses where people had passed on, and to keep a note of new births and marriages. There was a particularly sad visit when I discovered some five years after we had received such a warm welcome that Granny Baba had been hospitalised. I went to see her twice, and she made every effort to rally round, but she had become very weak, and indeed, she died not long afterwards. I was back in Tateyama by the time of the funeral, but I did send a telegram of greeting to the family, and they seemed appreciative. She had worked very hard to keep the house and family going after losing her son Sadami in the prime of his life, and she probably wore herself out, because she was considerably younger than several of the other grannies when she passed away.

During the hospital visits, when I took photographs of the children and some gifts deemed appropriate by the Kumagais where I was staying. I received gifts back, both from the Baba family, but even also from her doctor. It was about this time that I gradually became aware that the determination on the part of my closest friends there to keep giving me as much if not more than I could possibly manage to bring to them each time, was something I should relax and enjoy. Indeed, I decided to stop trying to keep up with them because they clearly cared more than I could about the debt being incurred by the latest recipient, so I eased off on the size and value of my gifts, and relations seemed to become a bit easier. It had been hard work to get all the first set of gifts for James home anyway!

On the second visit I made with the children, they were both attending primary school, and could speak quite passable Japanese, so it was a fun new experience for everyone. There were still few foreigners living in the Japanese countryside, so our arrival was again a remarkable event by local standards, and we were invited all over the place. I had settled into the seaside town again, this time to study the use of polite language, largely because the head of the kindergarten from our first visit was so skilled at it and encouraged my interest, but also because my friend Takako had secured us a house for the period, and we had built up a series of friends and contacts for the children. It was essential to make a visit to Kyushu again, which this time included a former student, Jenny, who had been helping me with the children, and Judy, an old friend from Oxford, but we were given our usual warm welcome.

My research on polite language did continue while I was in Kyushu, but with good periods of enjoyable time with Jenny, Judy and the children. Actually, polite language can be heard all the time wherever one finds oneself in Japan, so I never really stopped observing and making notes, but interestingly, people use it in different ways in different local dialects. I needed to formulate some questions to ask in the village, then, because it soon became clear that they use the polite expressions much more for ritual activities, such as weddings and funerals, than in everyday life, when I realised that they don't meet strangers enough to need the more distant language that I had been hearing in towns and cities. They had also adapted some of the regular polite expressions in ways that I didn't hear at all in standard Japanese, so the task became a bit more complicated than I had anticipated.

Fortuitously, the year after we returned to Oxford, I was invited back to Japan by my Tokyo professor to consider a position in a new university that was being set up in Niigata, a district on the north coast of the main island of Honshu. I was able to take enough time off from my job in Oxford to travel around the country and follow up some of the questions about regional variation that had remained after my period of research on polite language, and so this time I returned to Kurotsuchi without the friends and children who had quite reasonably distracted me then. It was good to have the time and space to do the research, but also to consolidate some other relationships, for example with the other lovely granny who had written regularly to me after I first returned,[12] and to hear all about the wedding of young Chika, whose mother had been dubious about her choice of spouse on my previous visit.

Considering the possibility of a job in Japan was partly to appease the demand on my professor to find someone who would be available if the university received permission from the government to set itself up – it needed contracted staff – but my continuing affair with the village, which had grown into a full-blown affair with Japan, had been quite detrimental to my marriage with Dennis. There were people – even back in those days – whose marriages survived such conflicting demands on the time and mutual support of the spouses, but ours sadly proved not to be one of them.

---

[12] See illustration on page 5.

Chapter Thirteen

International Links

AS the years went by, I returned reasonably regularly to Kurot-suchi. Of course, to keep in touch with everyone, but also to update my understanding of changing rural Japan because Japan in general had become my speciality as an anthropologist and I taught about it, wrote a textbook about Japanese society, and visited for various research projects. I eventually secured a full-time teaching job at Oxford Polytechnic, which became Oxford Brookes University, but only after a three-year stint at Stirling University where I contributed to an exciting development called the Scottish Centre for Japanese Studies. Sadly, it only lasted as long as Japan was the number one amazing Far Eastern economy, but the place I bought beside a cheerfully running burn in the Ochil Hills became my bolt hole for writing almost every summer after that, and later, the place where I would retire and entertain generations of Kumagais and other Japanese visitors, and self-isolate during the 2020 coronavirus pandemic when this book was finally completed!

Actually, my first contact with Kurotsuchi folk outside Kurotsuchi was with the eldest daughter of the shopkeeper, who I had not known very well in the village, but she married a man who worked for a big company, and her mother sent me to visit her as they travelled around. Our children were not too different in age, and we first visited them in Yokohama, then later, when they were sent to Toronto in Canada, they entertained us there, and they also visited me in Oxford. Mutsuko was the first Kumagai to visit Oxford, however, and she arrived just as I was organising to move a van of furniture to Scotland, so she travelled up via the Lake District, as she had loved *Swallows and Amazons* as a child and became our first visitor beside the burn. Later her parents would come too, but only after they retired, and together we drove back down the length of England so that they could spend time in London and Oxford as well. Atsushi came with his young wife, and so enjoyed cultural activities

Mrs Kumagai in London

such as eating haggis, visiting a whisky distillery, and striding about a local Highland Games in the rain that they returned kitted out in authentic Scottish bandsmen's coats.

The most unusual visit came about in a more convoluted way, but it has left a legacy of which I am particularly proud. During one of my visits to the village, I noticed that the house of a rather poor family had been rebuilt in a lavish and impressive style. The original house had been the home of a couple that made bamboo baskets, and who had kindly made little toys for my boys when they were visiting. It had been one of the smaller houses, so the new construction was very noticeable, and I called by to congratulate them. In fact, it was the son of the bamboo artist who had built the house; he had been one of the trainees at the friendly Satsue household when I was first in the village, and he had clearly graduated with flying colours. The bamboo artist and his wife were still there, they had retired on the strength of their son's success and they greeted me warmly.

It was around this time that we had been trying to raise money at Oxford Brookes to build a Japanese room for our students, and although we hadn't yet reached a high enough sum for the venture, it occurred to me that this talented Mr. Kawaguchi might make an excellent artist to carry out the job when we did achieve it. I raised the subject with him, and he was immediately interested. He took me round to see some of his other creations, which were largely traditional, but with new features, so I headed home with the idea firmly fixed in my head. It took three years to overcome all the related problems. Raising money was an important one, but there was the need to secure a location, and the powers-that-be at the university were worried about other things, like the fire risk, and the complications of hiring a foreigner, so it took a while to sort things out. I also had to negotiate how to import the relevant materials from Japan.

* * *

Eventually, we did build our room – in an abandoned branch of a bank, which happened to be in the very building where we had our offices – and Kiyotoshi Kawaguchi and his son Yuki gave generously of their time once I had arranged travel and their accommodation at my home. They had very little English, so they preferred to

Opening of Japanese room at Oxford Brookes University

stay with me, but the three weeks they spent installing the materials we had sent, in cooperation with a wonderful Oxford carpenter who had been employed to overcome one of the university's issues but could speak no Japanese, were some of the most exciting of my career. Staff and students who could speak Japanese were on hand to help at all times, we carried out the appropriate rituals, and there was generally a highly co-operative spirit among my colleagues in the building who were temporarily inconvenienced by the work. Although we had encountered considerable resistance during the planning process, members of the university at all levels were delighted with the result and the opening ceremony was a great moment of triumph!

Back in the village, there was an interesting reaction. That particular Kawaguchi family became firm friends, of course, especially as the carpenter's wife and cousin managed to visit Oxford while they were there, so we had some fun as well as completing the work. Another example of jealousy occurred, however, as the formerly friendly fishmonger's husband was also a carpenter, and he was evidently miffed that he had not been invited. He blanked me completely as I passed his workshop, and his wife simply pronounced my name and walked on when we met. Interestingly, the family of the former papermakers invited me round when we were collecting the materials and offered a beautiful hanging scroll for the *tokonoma* we planned to build in the room. One of Mihoko's daughters was preparing to study English on the Isle of Wight, so once the room was built, her parents found their way to the United Kingdom, and be-

Japanese room with Shibatas in it

came our next Kurotsuchi visitors. I hope they weren't discriminated against again (as they had been after the BBC visit), for the scroll is simply beautiful and reads – in elaborate Chinese characters – 'The Way of the Arts is Infinite'.

My students at the time of this building project had been excited and helpful, and one who had carried out fieldwork in a nearby part of Kyushu, particularly impressed the Kawaguchi carpenters as he could speak their dialect almost perfectly and enjoyed introducing them to some local pubs. I had called on Bruce during one of my visits to Japan, and we drove together over the rather steep and scary hills that separated his field site from mine. I didn't have time to stay in the village on that occasion, but we did pay a visit to Yame City Hall where Bruce was impressed to find that Fujita san (ref. Chapter 5) not only remembered me but spoke very positively about our experience working together. My old house in Kitoin had by this time been demolished, and the Kumagais had moved back into the family home on the border of Kurotsuchi, so we were only able to stand sadly at the site of my first residence.

In fact, visits around this time were a little sad altogether, as Japan's amazing economic bubble had burst, and chrysanthemum sales were apparently being undercut by cheaper flowers coming in from China and South Korea where wages were lower. The tea fields were still flourishing, but people from houses with

Bruce and carpenters in the pub

crafts and small businesses were also doing less well than they had, and more young people were tending to leave, rather than stay and work in the family home. There were still 50 houses in the village at the turn of the millennium (down from 54), but several were occupied by just one remaining person rather than whole families. Even where a son had agreed to stay and work, it had become difficult to find a wife who wanted to join a continuing house, partly because the practice of inviting a go-between to help was losing favour, and the age of marriage was rising. In Japan in general the birth rate was dropping and during my 2002 visit, only one child was attending primary school from Kurotsuchi.

My long-standing granny friend, Tomoe-san, was still alive, but had been admitted to a care home as she had become confused, according to her daughter-in-law, and tended to wander. Her son was also unwell, and only one of the three grandchildren was working at home, but had not yet found a wife. The two competent farm workers were very busy then, and could not cope with Tomoe as well, so reluctantly they had negotiated her care. We went to visit, and the surroundings seemed nice enough, but the residents did not look too cheerful. Tomoe did, I think, remember me, and she perked up as we walked around together, but she didn't seem very settled, and kept suggesting we 'go home'.

It had until that time been usual for daughters and daughters-in-law to take care of the elderly in a continuing house, and Hideshi and his wife had spent many years looking after his mother after she suffered a debilitating stroke, but it was now becoming common to seek outside care instead. Somewhat ironically, women in some of the houses were going out to work, and when I asked their occupations, they told me they were being employed as carers, but I suppose they did at least have their own income doing it that way. The carpenter's wife was one of those, and I think it was having paid work that enabled her to come and visit Oxford during the building of the room, and her parents-in-law were still managing by themselves anyway. In another house I visited at that time, a granny had just passed away aged 100, and she had been resident in her own home throughout her life. Her son, the head of the house, had three daughters and she had spoken to me on an earlier visit of the need to find a husband to come and live with them. At this point, there was one daughter still at home, with a child, and she explained that her husband was a filmmaker and travelled for work, so she spent a lot of time there, but I didn't get the impression that it was a long-term commitment.

Another interesting change beginning to happen at that time was that young wives, some of whom lived in the family homes, or nearby, were keen to take care of their own children, rather than leave them with the grandparents while they went out to the greenhouses, or the tea fields, as the previous generation had done. There was therefore a generation of women, of about my age as it happened, who had not looked after small children much at all. They had left their own with their mothers or fathers in law, but now that they had grandchildren, they were not needed for that role. When I asked them whether they felt sorry about this situation, they laughed and admitted that they were not too bothered not to have the care of their young grandchildren on their hands.

Actually, some continuing families that were still working together had arranged that the young family would take an apartment and 'commute' to the greenhouses. The young mothers did often come to work, but they took their children to a nursery, and later to school, before they set off. They were not resident in the village then, but they usually lived nearby, and this new custom probably partly explains why there were so few primary school children setting off from the village that year. Interestingly, family celebrations would still be held in the main home, and the usual decorations for Girls' Day on March 3rd would be set up there, for example. I wondered whether the young family would move back into the main house when their parents could no longer manage, as the Kumagais had done, but I probably won't be able to return long enough myself to witness that if it happens!

Girls' day decorations in a family's main home

A visit to Masamichi, the carpenter who had trained Kiyotoshi and whose wife had looked after the apprentices as well as her own burgeoning family, revealed that neighbours were no longer involved in the housebuilding as they had been when I (and the BBC) were there before. He explained that many of the villagers were now too busy with their own work outside to take off the days required, and the numbers had fallen some years before. It was now customary to hand over all the building work to professionals, although the rituals were still observed, and I noticed in one case that the celebration when the roof was complete was also attended by the neighbours. A gathering formed, as before, at the base of the house, and the carpenters threw rice cakes and bags of snacks off the roof at the appropriate moment. I did try to find a Shinto priest in the Oxford region to carry out the ground purification ceremony when we built the room there, but although my mission failed, the carpentry team just did it anyway, an event attended by my colleagues and some of the students in Japanese Studies.

One last call I made during the visit when we collected materials for the room was to the mayor of Yame City, who agreed to support our venture by adding some local products for the room. These included a lantern made of volcanic lava which we eventually placed in a tiny garden in front of the room outside, another was a lamp made of local paper which we placed in the *tokonoma* inside the room. Further locally made paper was used for the traditional paper walls or *shoji* used to decorate the inside of the room. Noda Kuniyoshi was the mayor at the time, and he later became a member of parliament for the area, so it was useful to have made his acquaintance and added a first-hand political element to the next update I would be asked to do for my textbook.

Chapter Fourteen

Party at the New Village Hall

VISITS after that rather sad one were much more positive as a growing interest in rural Japan was emerging, both by Japanese city dwellers, and by academics in Europe and elsewhere. It began quite slowly, but I couldn't help noticing interesting contrasts between the lives of my friends in Tokyo and the villagers in Kyushu. One of my friends working in another Japanese city had built herself a country retreat in the mountains, and as internet access made it possible to keep in touch with the wider world from all over the country, I found that some of her neighbours there had moved their main homes into the cleaner, fresher air and were enjoying the more relaxed life style. Elsewhere, whole families were setting up homes in the country so that their children could enjoy the advantages of rural life.

The first time I visited Kurotsuchi after building the Japanese room in Oxford, the carpenter's family was of course very welcoming. They wanted me to stay with them, and I did consider it as it was February and they had a wonderful wood-burning stove, but I felt a strong loyalty to the Kumagais and decided to put up with their colder house for the sake of our ongoing friendship. In fact, when I called – this was part of a longer trip to Japan to update my textbook – I discovered that Miyako's mother, the Hiroshima granny who had come to live in the Kitoin house, had just died, and my proposed arrival date coincided with her funeral. I offered immediately to stay elsewhere, but that seemed to be the wrong suggestion altogether, and I took a taxi from the station, rather than being picked up as usual, to join a splendid family dinner with several visiting relatives from Hiroshima. The cremation and its associated ritual had taken place earlier in the day, and my role, once dinner was

Sleeping in front of Kumagai granny's ashes

over was to sleep next to granny's ashes 'so that she won't be lonely'. It did seem a little creepy, but I was overcome with a sense of being accepted in this family, and of course, I complied.

Over the next couple of days, Hisako, the daughter I had not met since she was a teenager, flew in from Seattle where she and her husband had settled, accompanied by their two teenage (and very American) children, and Atsushi appeared from Nagasaki with his new wife. So, sleeping with the ashes became quite a communal affair, as we all lined up our futons side by side, and then in the daytime began to plan the Buddhist ceremonies that would take place in the home and continue the sending off of the granny's soul. The arrival of the Buddhist priest was quite amusing because Mr. Kumagai, now the senior member of the family, explained that they would need guidance as there were no elders left to help them. We all smiled at the idea that he was not yet an elder though well into his seventies. Another roast beef dinner was a highlight of this visit though we spent some time trying to find containers suitable for the Yorkshire puddings, which ended up being made in madeleine tins!

Over at Kawaguchi the carpenter house, I was treated to a lovely meal, surrounded by the burgeoning family. The younger of their two sons was working with his father, and living in an apartment built above the workshop, just across the road from the main house. Riki had married

Hisako (née Kumagai) and family

Atsushi Kumagai and family

first and already had three chil-children, one girl and a pair of twin boys, though his wife as-sured me that she was planning five! At a time when Japan was bewailing a disastrous drop in the birth-rate, this was one of the positive aspects of visiting the countryside, for the

Meal with carpenter's family

following day we spent four hours watching a lively concert at the clearly thriving nursery they all attended. Yuki, who came to Oxford with his father, had also married, and he and his wife were expecting their first child. He pronounced himself ready to be a hands-on father, a new phe-nomenon apparently influenced by David Beckham, and taking the coun-try by storm, certainly supported by the government as a possible way to alleviate the future problems the drop in birth-rate would surely see.

Elsewhere in the village, there was plenty of evidence of new gen-erations being born. I had arrived a couple of weeks before Girls' Day – or Dolls' Day – when families with daughters and granddaughters set up stands in their homes headed by a lord and lady and all the attendants and equipment for a high ranking wedding, and in this region, it is also customary to hang other hand-made symbols of the celebration, so the houses were full of colour.[13] I visited one house where the decorations were in place for the family of a son who had set up his own apartment,

Sushi decorated with the lord and lady of Girls' Day

but who all came back for the ceremony, as mentioned in the last chapter, and a couple of others where the younger generation was still living in the main home, but grandparents from the in-coming wife had made and sent decorative dolls. In one case I was invited to dinner,

---

[13] See illustration on page 102.

and the meal included a huge plate of *shirashizushi* (sushi laid out rather than wrapped up) decorated with edible versions of the lord and lady on top. The town of Fukushima in the centre of Yame holds a Dolls' Day Festival at this time of year, and many houses display the dolls and implements of the grandmothers, and the grandmothers of the grandmothers, which makes for a fascinating visit.

At the other end of the life-cycle, I was introduced to the *rōjinkai* (Old Folks Group) of the local area by the wife of the original honey family – now the great-granny as her son had not only returned to the village to continue and develop his father's honey business, but was working with his own son, who was living in the house with his wife and two young children. Great-granny was off duty at last from honey work, although I did find her weeding the front garden, but she took me out to join some of her age-mates in a game known as 'ground golf', essentially a development of putting, but around a rough earthy area rather than a green. I had recently been retired off from my teaching work, and they deemed me old enough to join the group, but I'm afraid I didn't manage to build up the skill they had all acquired in the two mornings I spent with them.

During that visit, I discovered that the old village hall had been replaced with a spanking new one,[14] and various villagers were keen to show it off to me. Each house had made a contribution to the cost, as they were able, and even the two Baba sons who lived elsewhere had made a donation to the community of their upbringing. The village head of the time decided to hold a gathering while I was staying, and he asked me if I would say a few words to everyone. It was a good opportunity to thank them for their ongoing cooperation, but I have to say that the experience was a bit daunting. We showed the BBC film again, which was certainly a highlight of the evening as many

Ground golf with honey granny

---

[14] See illustration on page 121.

young people had never seen it, and one new resident whom I hadn't met before, brought along a video camera of his own and filmed the occasion. I was introduced as 'the professor', which made me feel a bit uncomfortable as I am always learning when I go to Kurotsuchi, so I reassured them that I might be a professor in the UK, but I am always a student in Japan.

An exciting outcome of this visit was a wonderful gift I received for the Japan Room at Brookes from a seamstress in the village who found herself with an unused wedding kimono, brightly coloured and beautifully embroidered with cranes and turtles and other symbols of good fortune and long-life. Her daughter had just got herself married at last, at the age of 41, and her mother had been so relieved that she made her the garment, but then found that her daughter had purchased her own. She helped me pack it up carefully, and I took it down to the old post-office where I used to send and receive my mail back in the day when that was the only form of communication. A complicated form has to be filled in when sending parcels out of the country and I was a bit stumped when asked to assess the value of the contents, so I consulted the postmistress and we made a guess.

A few days later I received an amazing phone call from the port of Kobe. I had decided to send the parcel by sea mail as I would be away for a while and it was cheaper that way, but some highly responsible and evidently caring person in the port had picked up a potential problem. They rang me and explained that a garment that I had valued so highly would surely incur a heavy duty when it arrived in the UK, so why didn't we change the value in order to avoid this unwanted cost? It was

certainly a good idea as the colleagues at Brookes where I was sending it would be unlikely to want to fork out for a parcel they hadn't ordered, and I still remembered the sad experience of my poor father-in-law when we sent the lava lantern, so of course I agreed. It took

**The kimono at Oxford Brookes
Japanese room**

me some time, however, to believe that such a thing had happened – why would someone in the port take such trouble? Why would they even care? I can only imagine that they wanted to give me a good impression of Japan, and it was perhaps a woman who knew that wedding kimonos lose their value once they have been worn. Who knows? It was just one of those magical moments that sometimes happen during an affair!

There was a three-year gap before I called in on Kurotsuchi again, and this was a brief visit but exciting because I discovered quite fortuitously that I had arrived on the day they were holding the festival at the sacred tree. I had been staying in Kyoto for this Japanese visit, working at the Institute that my former student Bruce had been involved in setting up for foreign students, who were thereby able to study in Japan. It was pretty full time, along with some research I decided to do on what makes retired people (like myself) happy in Japan, but a team making a radio programme about seaweed production for the BBC asked me to interpet for them at a village in another nearby part of Kyushu. I therefore decided to make a slight detour on the way back and walked in to Kurotsuchi entirely unannounced.

Sitting in a little row beside the new village hall were a group of housewives preparing food to serve during the festivities, and there among them was Hitomi Kawaguchi, the wife of the carpenter who had come to build the room in Oxford. She was a little miffed I hadn't given her any warning of my arrival, but my time there was short, and it was so good to find that at last I could witness at least part of the festival for the *Shinboku* sacred tree,[15] more affectionately known as *Gorogorosan*, the God of Lightening, who had so influenced the identity of Kurotsuchi folk. It was nearly 40 years since I had first arrived in the village, and somehow I had failed to find the spring part of the festival so near it must have been to my arrival, and then I had missed the autumn handover, as described in Chapter 12, so this was a great, serendipitous bonus and another opportunity to greet all the community members who turned out for the occasion.

---

[15] See illustration on page 5.

Chapter Fifteen

Forty Years and Counting

THERE has of course been much change in this community over the past 40 years, indeed I recorded change as the years went by, and documented it in the chapter about rural life in the five editions of my textbook *Understanding Japanese Society*. Actually, the community was in the process of some considerable development when I first arrived, and it has of course continued to change, sometimes for the better, sometimes in quite a lamentable way. All communities change, and it is of course a complete myth sometimes put about that we anthropologists wrote about places that were relatively static until they were invaded by the outside world. It is true that I was the only foreigner to live in the area at the time of my first visit, but there had been much internal change over the centuries before I turned up, and the increase in foreigners – English teachers form one group, migrant workers another – seems actually to have produced remarkably little effect!

So, what has changed, and what has not? Referring back to my first chapter, I would like to say immediately that I now find the place quite beautiful. The BBC film crew helped me to see that when the programme they made introduced a small, but very charming village to their viewers; my son and his girlfriend reinforced the idea as they chose shots to create a context for the film they made when we went back together in 2019. I guess they were all looking for the attractive aspects whereas I had been too focused on the immediate untidiness in my search for a way to open communication with the inhabitants of the houses. I know now that people like their houses to face south, and they all have their own paths of approach, so that is why the road through the middle was a misguided place to judge. A photograph I took from the front of a house in 1975 even shows one of the last remaining thatched roof houses.

The road is now (and was then) the place where people who live alongside park their vehicles, then to enter their houses away from the

House front (away from the road) and a
thatched roof

road, but the biggest change in atmosphere if one chooses to *walk* along that thoroughfare, is that there are very few people about. There is no shop or public bath to walk to anymore, almost all the houses have been rebuilt with their own private bathrooms, and everyone drives around, even from their homes to their greenhouses on the periphery. There are people passing through, of course, but they are behind their steering wheels, and unless they stop to say hello, there is no informal chat. No rice-hulling house remains, with a small group of elderly women passing the time,[16] and Mrs. Ubiquitous, who used to jump out and ask me where I was going, sadly passed away.

Both of the shops closed some time ago. The tobacconist remained open for as long as the owner could manage, and although she gradually depleted her stock as she grew older, she was in the premises daily to exchange pleasantries and pass the time of day almost until she became bedridden. Now there remains only a drinks machine, but it is perhaps significant that one of the first people we did encounter as we walked through the centre was the shopkeeper's son, who used to deliver the propane gas to householders to power their bath heaters and their kitchen stoves. He was working at a garage at the back of a smart new house that now stands on that central corner, and he explained that it is occupied by his son's family. There is still some sense of continuity then, but in the case of this family, like others, the generations don't live together as they did in the past.

The fishmonger's shop closed some years ago too, but her family still occupies the first buildings on both sides of the road as one enters the village from the main trunk road. The shop building still stands, but it is closed up, whereas on the other side of the road a colourful cluster of

---

[16] See illustration on page 3.

new buildings rises two stories around a car park, and apparently houses an old folks' home, run by her daughter and grandson. This was an incoming family, with a distinct surname from the majority of villagers, but it seems they have settled well and exhibit a strong sense of continuity despite still occupying quite a peripheral location. Once the now-old lady realised I was back in the area, she popped out again to greet me when she saw me, just as she had often done in the past, the carpentry rivalry apparently forgotten.

Fishmonger's new development, with ex-fishmonger

Continuity was a characteristic of almost all the families when I first arrived, and the houses were handed down through the generations, sometimes rebuilt as a young couple married and committed themselves to staying with their parents and grandparents. In those days, it would be a cause for much discussion and speculation if no one remained in the house to carry on the work of the family. Now a series of *ad hoc* relations have emerged in different cases, and it requires a bit more digging and investigation to unearth the way in which family ties are maintained. Some of the most successful houses when I was first in the village are now sadly occupied by only one remaining person, others that had been less well-off have consolidated and even grown.

The overall population has changed too. The 54 houses have become 45, and the numbers of farmers/horticulturalists has diminished slightly, although the greenhouses, which used to be covered in vast sheets of flapping plastic are now all trim, properly finished glasshouses. The dirt tracks that used to run out of the boundaries of the village and be maintained by hand regularly by groups comprising a representative of each of the houses, have been finished with tarmacadam, and the cars and trucks that run along them are big and shiny. During my first visit, there

Smart house with a tiled roof

were three old houses with thatched rooves, and one very scrappy-looking hut just outside the boundary. Now all the houses look very well maintained, if not regularly rebuilt, and several sport splendid tiled rooves. Indeed, one large house was being refurbished on the inside during our visit.

The chrysanthemums still provide a good income for several houses then, and the tea fields, also recently opened up when I first arrived, have now become a mark of prosperity for the whole area. In the city hall of Yame, to which the village still belongs administratively, there are photographs of the tea fields that have extended over much of the surrounding hillside, and the local tourist information centre sports shelf upon shelf of different varieties of tea for sale. When we went up to take a look at the *pairotto* ('pilot') where I had done some of my earliest fieldwork, we found a golden bust of Mr. Nishie, the local politician who

The tea fields, with film-maker Nadine posing during my last visit in 2019

Golden bust of Mr Nishie

• • •

had suggested the idea of opening up the common land, and who had indeed introduced me to the village in the first place.

Another interesting change is to be found in the crafts that are practised in the village. The carpenter who I persuaded to come to Oxford to build a Japanese room at my university is still there, and his son and family still live just across the road above the workshop; indeed, this was the second place where we found someone to greet as we walked about the village on first arrival. The son was actually tending his motor bike, but he reported that he now has four children, so still bucking the trend in Japan for the birth rate to be falling alarmingly. It was only a bit later when we were filming in the shrine that we noticed the huge, high extension that had been built above and behind the workshop. Plenty of space for his expanding family then, and a wonderful development of the tumbledown shed that had been the workshop of his bamboo-crafting grandfather. The only place where we found bamboo craft being practised in 2019 was in the Traditional Craft Centre which stands next to the Tourist Information Centre, again in the centre of Yame.

In the end we spent some time in the Craft Centre because it has on display all the crafts that used to be practised on a daily basis in the village, and which are now apparently a draw for the tourists encouraged to come to this area. Paper-making – which used in the past to occupy 30 houses in the village – was abandoned shortly after I visited with the BBC and filmed the last house practising it in 1979. As explained in the film, the family had three daughters and no sons, and although all three had learned the skills of creating hand-made paper, they had not managed to find an incoming husband who would do the same and the family had turned to horticulture. This is the family that donated the beautiful scroll we have hanging in the Japanese room at Oxford Brookes,[17] and they are now one of the most successful producers of chrysanthemums in the village, employing three Vietnamese girls to do much of the repetitive work in the greenhouses.

Lantern-making had been another skill practised in one of the homes, and this was also caught on the BBC depiction of the village. It is actually another use of the abundantly available bamboo, which is cut

---

[17] See illustration on page 100.

and curved into shape and then covered in delicate sheets of paper, so illustrating a combination of two of the other skills developed in the area. We filmed lanterns again this time, but only a display in the Craft Centre, rather than work in the home. The related change that has developed over the years introducing professional carers – both the carpenter's wife and his other son practice this profession – has replaced an almost inevitable responsibility for care in the home, and the footage of the lantern makers clearly depicted a member of the family with what is now called special needs sitting with the craftspeople at work.

Another well-known local product that used to be made by one housewife in the village is known as Kurume *gasuri*, a rather cheerfully decorated woven cloth which was used for women's work clothes, but which has now become sought after and fashionable even in an international context. There were some examples on sale in the Craft Centre, but they were very expensive, and I noticed that the factory in the neighbouring community that used to employ some of the other villagers to make this cloth had also closed down, so perhaps it is harder to come by than it used to be. The seamstress who used to make kimono, and who donated the one that we now display in our Japanese room at Brookes, is still there – we called on her – but she is retired, surrounded by yapping dogs, and has also given up the work. I took her a little china thimble with a picture of Oxford on it, but she didn't look especially impressed!

So, are there some new occupations? Some new crafts to report, apart from the caring we introduced in passing? To be honest I didn't find too many, but there are several new buildings in the village, and a couple of these house ongoing activities that must certainly bring in an income for the families concerned. One of them we visited almost by chance, as I wanted to have a word with the man who had recently become the new head of the village, about the family trees I was leaving with them. He and his wife were working together in a small factory full of machines that seemed to be producing plastic bags of various sizes. Plastic bags! What a come down from the beautiful crafts of the previous generation. This man and his father had been marketing paper when I first went there, rather than doing any particular craft themselves, and as

Mr. Kumagai reported, even machine-made paper is used less now. I found this new occupation a bit sad, for Japan uses a truly lamentable number of plastic bags, but I suppose the son had found a new way of making a living now if their old business was failing.

In fact, both these men – father and son – were university-educated, and described themselves as businessmen, so there is some continuity here too. I should perhaps be pleased to find businessmen making a living in this rural community, for one of the thriving big houses I had often visited during my first stay had lamented the fact that their son had done so well at school that he had gone off to university rather than staying in the family home to farm. He had gained a place at one of the big national universities – in Osaka – and had gone on to get a job with a prestigious company and never returned for more than holiday visits to the home of his birth. Now, forty years later, many Japanese city dwellers are looking with envy at rural life, and some are even working out ways to get back – so perhaps our new village head should be admired – even if he is making a living by producing such an environmentally unfriendly product!

Another shiny new building has been constructed on the site of the lovely old house where we stayed with the Baba family when I first returned with my children, a choice encouraged by everyone to cheer this elderly couple who had lost the whole succeeding generation when their son died. For several of my return visits after that their house had just been a tumble-down empty place once the old couple died, though as mentioned in the last chapter, I did notice that the two younger sons who had moved away had made donations to the new village hall. It seems they had sold the land by the time of my last visit, though, for this big new building was to be a cleaning business, and perhaps a home would be constructed nearby too, the neighbours suggested.

The outgoing head of the village with whom I had arranged to return with the family trees also runs a business, and in this case the farming family he grew up in has been continued in an interesting modern way. Again, a graduate, this time from Kyoto, another high-ranking national university, he worked for some years away from the village, but returned to build a beautiful new house beside the old family one and set

Yukio Kawaguchi's office, with daughter and son-in-law's house

up an office right there in front of it. He has three daughters and one of them married a young man who came into the business and built another new house for his own young family, there on the same plot. In this case, then, the family continues, they work together, but they live in separate buildings. They also maintain an interesting relationship with another of Yame's famous products, namely the stone lanterns which are fashioned using this company's tools from the resilient stone lava, spewed many years ago from Mount Aso, one of Kyushu's famous volcanos.

Chapter Sixteen

The End of the Affair

LONG-TERM relationships are usually marked by a collection of memorabilia which can be extracted from their places of safe-keeping and examined with variable measures of pleasure and sadness depending on the way things worked out over the years. I have collected many things over those 45 years, but the penultimate time I returned to the village, a trip from Hokkaido to Okinawa to update my textbook, I had been unable before I left to locate that all-important notebook of information about each of the families, and my memory had not served me as well as it should have. Some people are etched firmly in my mind, but it was very frustrating to hear sadness being expressed about someone who had recently died, but not be able to remember who they were, or to which house they had belonged. Until then I had made a point wherever possible of visiting the household Buddhist altar in the homes of people who died since my previous visits, lighting a couple of sticks of incense, ringing the bell, and thereby ritually saying farewell to them. I felt bad about being unable to complete the task on that occasion, and I think it was partly that lapse that gave me the idea of executing some kind of farewell to the community. I may return one day – the brief visit I mentioned in Chapter 14 was entirely unplanned as I just happened to be passing nearby – but I thought it would be good to be able to draw a line under the ongoing investigations I had been carrying out up to that time.

In any case, I had informed the publisher that this would be my last update of the *Understanding Japanese Society* textbook, and I had handed over all my old photographic slides of the village to the Pitt Rivers Museum as a collection to be digitalised and then archived, so it seemed to make sense to find a way to bring my 'affair with the village' to a close as well. It is also a good thing these days to offer some kind of return to the place where we anthropologists have worked. In the past, when it was more difficult to travel long distances, especially into rural locations, anthropologists sometimes failed altogether to return, and some of the people about whom work has been published, even become famous, quite rightly feel neglected. Indigenous Peoples sometimes even claim angrily that their knowledge was stolen from them, though they may also be pleased it has not been lost.

Japanese villagers have not made complaints such as these, as far as I know, and I have of course returned several times. I also sent copies of the books I have written using village materials, but they are in English, and although some effort was made to have the first one translated, the project seems not to have been completed. I have collected large quantities of notes during my stays, but these are also in English, and in my rather poor hand-writing, so I didn't think the villagers would be interested in them. On the other hand, the detailed family trees I made for all of the houses were written using the *kanji* that the people themselves recognise for their names, so I decided that they would be a better thing to offer to hand over, along with charts showing where incoming wives and adopted husbands had come from, as well as destinations of those who had left. The large village-wide chart of all the families, showing who was related to whom, would also be of much more interest to them than to my descendants, I thought, so I consulted the head of the village during the updating visit in 2017 and he agreed that they would like to receive them. I did have a slight niggling doubt about the source of some of my information as it had been a normally inaccessible archive of the Yame City Hall, but they had during my first stay agreed to let me study their records, as long as each house signed (and sealed – in Japanese fashion) their agreement. This they had done, so I therefore decided to go ahead with the plan and hope that no future generations would be upset by any information they found there.

Once I secured funding from the Daiwa Foundation for this hand-over visit, I sent an e-mail to the man who had been the Village Head in 2017, and he confirmed that he would be available during the planned period in 2019, so his office was my first port of call on arrival. He was out until the evening, as he had warned, but the office staff were expecting me, and we fixed a time for me to call by later. The meeting was positive, and friendly. I was carrying the documents, and briefly laid them out on his table, but he proposed asking the village officials to meet in the Village Hall at a suitable time, and then I could hand them over properly. This suited me fine, and my son was anyway keen to film a formal handover, so we made

Photo taken outside the village hall at the handover

a date, which he confirmed as we sat there by calling his fellow officials, and the time was entered in our diaries. The role of Village Head is actually a circulating one, so this had now been passed on, but the new Head was happy to leave these arrangements to his predecessor, and ready to turn out on the day we had fixed.

I had also proposed to the Daiwa Foundation that people might like to meet in the Village Hall to see their own family components, and perhaps to update them, but although everyone expressed delight at the overall chart I had made – perhaps even if only to admire the Japanese script I had managed to reproduce for names they had themselves forgotten – I did not actually find anyone interested enough to engage in the updating process. The Kumagais, who now live just over the border in the next community, reminded me that Kurotsuchi people are known for their hard work – they are *gamadashimono* in local dialect – so giving up work time to update their family trees probably wouldn't be a priority. I decided instead then to visit as many houses as possible, simply to show them their own charts, and offer to make copies for them – or let them make their own, as it worked out – and this decision resulted in a series of less well-planned but very fine activities with which to mark the formal end of my affair with the occupants of this village. It reminded me a little of the visits I had made to each house to get their permission to study their records in the first place. My son and his girlfriend filmed most of what I did so we now have a nice documentary of this last visit, which the villagers have seen and admired.

● ● ●

Children playing on swings

Many of these visits were unre-markable, although pleasant and quite nostalgic, but in all cases, we referred to earlier events we had taken part in to-gether, and as we filmed many of these discussions, some of the stories make nice footage. We also filmed the two sacred spots in the village and remem-bered, using old still photographs in the film, former events that had taken place there: the annual festival at the Ten-mangu Shrine,[18] the presentation to the local guardian deity of babies[19] and brides, and playing with children on the swings. At the Shrine to the God of Lightening, which is now also the location of the new Village Hall, I had watched people play games of various sorts – badminton, gate ball and baseball – and we caught some children playing tag for the film.

We also collected film of ongoing daily activities, and sometimes these escalated into more interesting events, in one case illustrating a typ-ical kind of frustration I had quite often experienced during my years of research. We were passing the house of Hideshi Shibata, the man whose wedding photograph had appeared on the front of my first book, and they were busy sorting their crop of newly picked chrysanthemums into bundles ready to take to the Cooperative for sale. They had installed quite an impressive sorting machine in their front workshop to speed up the job, and I chatted with Tomiko, his wife, as the machine and the filmmakers did their work. I asked after their three adult children and the grandchildren, and she encouraged us to come back later 'to look at some photographs'. We were already booked for that evening so I settled on the following one, and as the film-makers thought looking at photographs something they could miss, I went alone. Well, that was a typically un-scripted mistake of the sort I used to weep about, for all of their seven

[18] See illustration on page 3.
[19] See illustration on pages 30 and 31.

grandchildren had been assembled, along with some of their parents, and they were deeply disappointed to find that my albeit meagre offspring had gone off to cook their evening meal. Moreover, they had probably been promised becoming stars of our film.

Three of my books I had sent them, which happened to have members of these families in photographs on the cover, were laid out on the table, alongside a lovely album the family had made of their grandparents celebrating sixty years of age. This is the time known as *kanreki* when the year in the Chinese/Japanese calendar in which people were born makes its first return, and in some cases, including this one, rather splendid red garments are purchased and worn as an expression of a symbolic return to childhood. So, the photographs turned out to be rather special too. Well, I looked at them, and took photographs of my own of the books and the assembled bevy of youngsters, but I was not really a good substitute for the video camera, and in the end we made a date for the following weekend when the children would be free to come again, and there would be more daylight for filming. The situation was eventually saved, then, but I did appeal again sadly, as I had done many times in the past, 'Why didn't you let me know (in this case, that you had invited everyone to come around)?'

A much more neatly arranged follow-up visit was to see where the bee hives had been brought down from the mountains for the winter. This was particularly nostalgic, as the honey family, as I had always called them, had taken me out on just such an exercise when I was first in the village, and this was another family that had grown and thrived since that original stay, when the young son had given me a lift to Fukuoka University. The grandmother who had tak-

Shibata Hideshi and family with my books on display

en me out to play a game of 'ground golf' with the old folks' club, was sadly in a care home during this last visit, and I didn't get around to visiting her, but her son and grandson were going up to check on the hives, and we followed them in our vehicle so we could film what they were doing. It was quite a performance as we all had to wear wellington boots and protective clothing, including netting helmets over our heads, and they had been a little optimistic about the size of trousers I would need! It all worked out eventually, however, and we watched and filmed a selection of the hives being opened and checked, and the substitute sugar solution being given to the bees, this being a process which continues throughout the winter.

Another family we called upon, also a couple whose wedding I had attended the first time, had also done extremely well with their business. This time it was mostly chrysanthemum cultivation, and the house on the edge of the village beyond the shrine, is now surrounded by large greenhouses in the immediate vicinity. The family home itself had been rebuilt a dozen years before, a huge impressive building with a splendid roof, and rather unusually, quite a pretty garden adorning the area around the front door. Here too, the generations are working together, and the son of the couple I had seen wed, was at work. However, we encountered a downside to all this prosperity that day, for the greenhouses were open and he was administering an abundant spray treatment, which I thought at first might be water as he was wearing no protection, but it turned out to be pesticide. The air was thick with the small of chlorine, we soon noticed, and we decided to leave their family tree with them and return to chat later.

No one had ever claimed that the horticulture was achieved organically, indeed use of bud-pruning and elaborate electric lighting was already interfering with any natural cycles the plants might have had, but we were shocked that no one bothered to wear a face mask or close the greenhouses to protect the surrounding environment. Returning later that day to the Kumagais, we discovered that this abundant rather careless use of pesticides is a bit of a problem locally. The Kumagais themselves grow vegetables as a hobby, and as a source of good – and in their case organic – food. Their vegetables are delicious – we were treated to much lovely food daily – but they did concede that the whole water table in the area is polluted with the pesticide that is used so freely by the chrysanthemum cultivators. The tea fields are also sprayed regularly, as are the rice fields, so living in this countryside turns out actually to be far from the healthy experience some city folk are trying to create in other less financially successful parts of rural Japan.

Perhaps this air pollution was one of the causes of a persistent dizziness I experienced during this visit? It could also have been that I am now just too old to get up and down from sleeping and eating on the tatami matting that I used to do so cheerfully when I was younger. Whatever it was, it disappeared as soon as I boarded my flight back to the UK. I don't think I am quite ready to join the care home my friend from the honey family has been assigned, but I don't feel too bad about bringing this wonderful affair to an end, and I was relieved when the village officials produced a small chair for me to sit on for the hand-over of the documents. I would have spurned it scornfully during my until then persistent attempts to do the anthropological thing and live as the locals do, but I felt comfortable that I had found a way formally to hand over a part of what had made my career in anthropology reasonably successful to representatives of those who had played such an important part in that achievement.

Epilogue

TWO of the Kumagai children, who had played such an interesting part in our lives when Dennis and I were living next door to them, returned during this last visit, and we decided to film some discussion of our memories of the time. The house Dennis and I had shared was demolished some years before, but the spot is still vacant, and we could even discern the remains of the garden and its pond. The Kumagai paper-making factory stands empty now that they have retired, and the old house has also been abandoned since the wife's mother, who moved in when they took over the main family home, passed on. So, we gathered, perhaps a little forlornly at first, to recreate some of our memories, but as it happened, it turned out to be quite fun. Atsushi, the youngest son and now one of Japan's best-known specialists in radiation sickness, had come with his own son, by chance approximately the same age at two years old as he had himself been at the time, and the youngest Kumagai explored the surrounding land just as his father had done at that earlier time. Although at first claiming he remembered little, Atsushi began to recall the door he used to leave at his own house, and the path through the scrub at the back that he had taken to visit me, which he did quite often when I was working there.

The girls used to come for English lessons with Dennis, and Mutsuko recalled some of the phrases he had had her practice and repeat. We all remembered the roast beef dinner, but she also remembered his instructions about not slurping when eating spaghetti bolognaise, unlike the noisy polite way one eats noodles in Japan! In fact, the whole Kumagai family recalled with pleasure and nostalgia the experience of having an anthropologist come and live next door, even if it was only for a year, and they had apparently referred to the room where I stayed after Dennis left as Hendry-san's room long after we had gone.

These nostalgic musings are recorded, along with elements of the whole story recounted here, in the *Leaf of Life* film made by my son James and his partner Nadine Kreter.

Image Credits

The illustrations in this book are sourced from the personal photographic collection of the author, but the earlier images have been donated to the Pitt Rivers Museum, University of Oxford, which holds the copyright in perpetuity, as detailed below. The other exceptions are also listed below:

Frontispiece: Image by Daniel Diaz at Pixabay. Public Domain Image.

Map: Image by Gerd Altmann at Pixabay. Public Domain Image.

Page 1: Copyright © Pitt Rivers Museum, University of Oxford. Accession Number: 2016.16.3271.

Page 3: Copyright © Pitt Rivers Museum, University of Oxford. Accession Numbers: 2016.16.3275 (top image), 2016.16.347 (bottom image).

Page 4: Copyright © Pitt Rivers Museum, University of Oxford. Accession Number: 2016.16.484.

Page 5: Copyright © Pitt Rivers Museum, University of Oxford. Accession Number: 2016.16.3422 (top image), 2016.16.3393 (bottom-left image), 2016.16.712 (bottom-right image).

Page 6: Copyright © Pitt Rivers Museum, University of Oxford. Accession Number: 2016.16.3401 (top image), 2016.16.3399 (bottom image).

Page 7: Copyright © Pitt Rivers Museum, University of Oxford. Accession Number: 2016.16.3280 (top-left image), 2016.16.3287 (top-right image), 2016.16.3297 (bottom image).

Page 10: Copyright © Pitt Rivers Museum, University of Oxford. Accession Number: 2016.16.358 (top image), 2016.16.300 (bottom image).

Page 13: Copyright © Pitt Rivers Museum, University of Oxford. Accession Number: 2016.16.725.

Page 19: Copyright © Pitt Rivers Museum, University of Oxford. Accession Number: 2016.16.324.

Page 20: Copyright © Pitt Rivers Museum, University of Oxford. Accession Number: 2016.16.3411.

Page 26: Copyright © Pitt Rivers Museum, University of

Oxford. Accession Number: 2016.16.3424.

Page 121: Copyright © Leaf of Life Films, and reproduced by kind courtesy of the copyright holder.

About the Author

JOY HENDRY was born in Birmingham, brought up within a Scottish community in Warwickshire, travelling back to the home country every summer to visit relatives and enjoy the wonderful opportunities for hiking and camping. She was also sometimes sent, alone from quite an early age, to visit her mother's relatives in Yorkshire, where her aunt introduced her to beachcombing and coastal walks and encouraged her ambition to become a writer. From the age of nine, Joy attended Penrhos College, a girls' boarding school by the sea in North Wales, advised (correctly) by the family doctor to help her recover from a long and quite debilitating attack of sinusitis. Travel, adventure and new experiences were thus woven into her upbringing, and possibly underpinned her eventual choice of social anthropology as a career.

Before she discovered that path, she took a first degree in General Science at Kings College, London, in the heart of the swinging sixties, then travelled and worked as a teacher and a journalist in Canada and Mexico. She first sailed into Japan on a cruise ship making its way from Brazil to Yokohama Bay in the spring of 1971 to fulfil an ambition sparked by a visit to the Japanese pavilion at the 1967 EXPO in Montreal to learn the Japanese language. Boarding this liner in Los Angeles she had nearly three weeks to meet people and stumble through early linguistic infelicities before she disembarked, useful in a country still quite sparse in foreign visitors. The next six months were spent attending language school, living with a group of young Japanese who became lifelong friends, and travelling from the northernmost tip to the south of the four main islands with one Yasuro-san who also appears in the present volume.

Joy went back to university to study social anthropology at Lady Margaret Hall, Oxford, in the autumn of that same year, and began the story that this volume recounts during that period of training. She met her husband Dennis in Oxford, and he and their two sons, James and William, joined her in Japan for some of her fieldwork, as also recounted in this volume; otherwise they made their home in the city of Morse and the Dreaming Spires, and she now (when possible) divides her time between these two locations. She went on to teach for many years at Oxford Brookes University and after retirement was made an emeritus professor. She also held a readership in the Scottish Centre for Japanese Studies at the University of Stirling from 1989-92, when she established a home in Tillicoultry, Clackmannanshire, where she would return most summers to write. Now released from teaching, this same activity has enabled her to spend the 2020 lockdown period in relative peace and comfort.

Joy also founded a global professional organisation called the Japan Anthropology Workshop and another, the Europe Japan Research Centre, largely based at Oxford Brookes, where she helped to found one of the most successful departments of Japanese in the UK. She has been president of the British Association for Japanese Studies, vice president of the European Association for Japanese Studies, and in 2017, the Government of Japan bestowed on her the Order of the Rising Sun, Gold Rays with Rosette, "in recognition of her outstanding contribution to the promotion of Japanese Studies in the UK and thus to deeper mutual understanding between Japan and the United Kingdom".

Not all Joy's research has been in Japan, however, and her initial interest in World Fairs, also sparked by the EXPO in Montreal in

1967, led much later to projects on cultural display which started in Japanese gardens and theme parks, but eventually led to eight months among First Nations in Canada and three and four months respectively with Aboriginal scholars in Australia and Maori in New Zealand. The Canadian research was about cultural education centres set up by members of Canada's First Peoples to represent themselves rather than be displayed in European-style museums, and she lived on a Reserve with a Mohawk/Seneca family whose son-in-law had (by serendipitous chance) set up the Native Pavilion in Montreal that had not only inspired Joy, but also convinced the Canadian government to fund many ensuing projects. Her Indigenous friends often claim Scottish ancestry, but the second study, supported by the University of Melbourne in Australia and the University of Otago, Dunedin, New Zealand, was about people seeking recognition for an indigenous science that pre-dates the findings of the Scottish Enlightenment that were carried to their lands by those antecedents.

Already author of two textbooks on the subject of social anthropology, Joy is now working to broaden public interest in the discipline, and she devised the four units offered by the Scottish Qualifications Authority to schools and colleges in Scotland, and when invited, gives talks and lectures on the subject, as well as on Japan. Since the extended lockdown of 2020 she has been working on a first novel set in Mexico, the place where she herself first discovered the subject.

Some aspects of the Affair with the Village were filmed by Joy's son James and his partner Nadine Kreter in 2019 and can be viewed on YouTube under the title *Understanding Japanese Culture* (Leaf of Life films).

The Heart 200 Book

A Companion Guide to Scotland's Most Exciting Road Trip

By Thomas A. Christie and Julie Christie

The Heart 200 route is a unique road trip around some of the most beautiful locations in Central Scotland. Two hundred miles running through Stirlingshire and Perthshire, Heart 200 takes its visitors on an epic adventure to suit every taste—whether you are an outdoors enthusiast, an aficionado of history, or simply looking to enjoy yourself in some of the most stunning natural surroundings in the world.

Written with the full approval and co-operation of the Heart 200 team, *The Heart 200 Book* is a guide to the very best that the route has to offer. You will discover the history and culture of this remarkable region, from antiquity to the modern day, with more than a few unexpected insights along the way. Over the millennia, this amazing land has made its mark on world history thanks to famous figures ranging from the ancient Celts and the Roman Empire to King Robert the Bruce and Mary Queen of Scots, by way of Bonnie Prince Charlie, Rob Roy MacGregor, Robert Burns, Sir Walter Scott, Queen Victoria and even The Beatles!

So whether you're travelling by foot, car, motorhome or bike, get ready for a journey like no other as the Heart 200 invites you to encounter standing stones and steamships, castles and chocolatiers, watersports and whisky distilleries... and surprising secrets aplenty! Illustrated with full-colour photography and complete with Internet hyperlinks to accompany the attractions, *The Heart 200 Book* will introduce you to some of the most remarkable places in all of Scotland and encourage you to experience each and every one for yourself. It really will be a tour that you'll never forget.

For details of new and forthcoming books from
Extremis Publishing, including our monthly podcast,
please visit our official website at:

www.extremispublishing.com

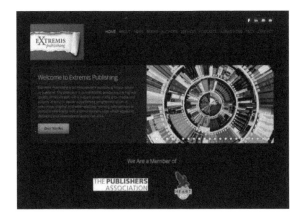

or follow us on social media at:

www.facebook.com/extremispublishing

www.linkedin.com/company/extremis-publishing-ltd-/

Lightning Source UK Ltd.
Milton Keynes UK
UKHW050718250521
384331UK00002BA/5